BBC
Speakout
3RD EDITION

A1

Split 1
Units 1–4

Student's Book and eBook

Speakout | 3RD EDITION | CONTENTS | A1 Split 1

LESSON	GRAMMAR/FUNCTION	VOCABULARY	PRONUNCIATION
LEAD-IN p6			

1 welcome! BBC VLOGS | Where are you from?

LESSON	GRAMMAR/FUNCTION	VOCABULARY	PRONUNCIATION
1A Hello p8	Present simple *be*: *I, you*	Hello and goodbye; countries and nationalities	Intonation in greetings
1B Two jobs p10	Present simple *be*: *he, she, it*	Jobs	Word stress in jobs
1C Checking in p12	How to … ask and answer simple questions	The alphabet	The alphabet
1D What's your name? p14	Singular and plural nouns; *a, an*; *have, has*	Common objects	

UNIT 1 REVIEW p16   SOUNDS AND SPELLING syllables, stress and /ə/; /s/, /z/, /ɪz/ in plurals

2 people BBC VLOGS | Where are you now?

LESSON	GRAMMAR/FUNCTION	VOCABULARY	PRONUNCIATION
2A Where are they? p18	Present simple *be*: *we, you, they*	Numbers 11–100; common adjectives (1)	Word stress in numbers
2B Family and friends p20	Possessive adjectives	Family; people	Syllables
2C Small talk p22	How to … have short conversations	Feelings	Stress in phrases **FUTURE SKILLS** Self-management
2D Best Home Cook p24	*wh-* questions + *be*		

UNIT 2 REVIEW p26   SOUNDS AND SPELLING short and long sounds (1): /ɪ/, /iː/, /ʊ/, /uː/; /w/ and /h/ in question words

3 things BBC VLOGS | What's your favourite thing?

LESSON	GRAMMAR/FUNCTION	VOCABULARY	PRONUNCIATION
3A Favourites p28	Possessive *'s*	Things; colours	Possessive *'s*
3B What's on your desk? p30	Present simple *have* + *yes/no* questions (*I, you, we, they*)	Desk objects	Sentence stress
3C How much is it? p32	How to … shop for clothes	Clothes	Intonation
3D Shopping p34	Likes, dislikes and opinions	Shops	

UNIT 3 REVIEW p36   SOUNDS AND SPELLING voiced and unvoiced consonants (1): /p/ and /b/, /k/ and /g/, /t/ and /d/; sounds

4 every day BBC VLOGS | What's your favourite meal of the day – breakfast, lunch or dinner?

LESSON	GRAMMAR/FUNCTION	VOCABULARY	PRONUNCIATION
4A Time for lunch! p38	Adverbs of frequency	Food and drink	Word stress
4B A day in the life p40	Present simple: regular verbs (*he, she, it*)	Everyday activities (1); telling the time	Third person *-s*
4C Can I have … ? p42	How to … order in a café	Café words	Intonation in *or* phrases
4D Earth From Space p44	Present simple: *yes/no* questions (*he, she, it*)		

UNIT 4 REVIEW p46   SOUNDS AND SPELLING short vowels: /e/, /æ/, /ʌ/; *does*: /dʌz/ or /dəz/?

WRITING BANK p88   **GRAMMAR BANK** p92   **VOCABULARY BANK** p124   **COMMUNICATION BANK** p140

READING	LISTENING/VIDEO	SPEAKING	WRITING
	Understand people saying 'hello'	Introduce yourself	Write a chat message to introduce yourself; use capital letters, full stops and question marks
Read an article about people with two jobs		Talk about people and their jobs	
	Understand people asking and answering simple questions	Ask and answer simple questions **FUTURE SKILLS** Self-management	
	BBC Street Interviews about what's in your bag	Talk about what's in your bag	Write a lost and found post
Read a blog about two people		Talk about groups of people	
	Understand someone talking about their family around the world	Talk about your friends and family	Write a description of a photo; use *and*
	Understand short conversations	Have short conversations	
	BBC Programme *Best Home Cook*	Ask about three people	Write a message about a friend
Read a blog about people's favourite things		Talk about people's things	Write about favourite things; use *and*, *but*
	Understand a radio phone-in about people's desks	Talk about your desk **FUTURE SKILLS** Collaboration	
	Understand conversations about shopping for clothes	Have shopping conversations	
	BBC Street Interviews about people's shopping habits	Ask and answer questions	Write a personal profile
	Understand people from different countries talking about lunch	Talk about food	Write an email to a friend
Read an article about an influencer's daily routine		Ask and answer about your daily routine	
	Understand conversations in a café	Order in a café	
	BBC Programme *Earth From Space*	Ask about someone's routine	Write a quiz

SOUNDS AND SPELLING p151   **AUDIOSCRIPTS** p162   **VIDEOSCRIPTS** p172   **VERB TABLE** p175

Speakout | 3RD EDITION | CONTENTS | A1 Split 2

LESSON	GRAMMAR/FUNCTION	VOCABULARY	PRONUNCIATION
5 action BBC VLOGS | Tell me about your job.			
5A Good colleagues p48	Object pronouns	Common verbs (1) **FUTURE SKILLS** Self-management	Linking with object pronouns
5B Yes, I can! p50	*can* for ability	Verbs of ability	*can*: weak and strong forms
5C Can you help me? p52	**How to …** make requests and offers	Common adjectives (2)	Weak forms: *could you*
5D Birthday! p54	Ordinal numbers; dates	Months	

UNIT 5 REVIEW p56   **SOUNDS AND SPELLING** voiced and unvoiced consonants (2): /f/ and /v/, /θ/ and /ð/; silent *e* (1): /ɪ/ to /aɪ/

LESSON	GRAMMAR/FUNCTION	VOCABULARY	PRONUNCIATION
6 where? BBC VLOGS | Where are you and what can you see?			
6A Lost p58	Prepositions of place	Rooms and furniture **FUTURE SKILLS** Self-management	Sentence stress
6B A great place to live p60	*there is, there are*	Places in town (1)	Linking with *there*
6C Where are you? p62	**How to …** ask where a place is	Places in town (2); signs in buildings	Weak forms with *to, of* and *the*
6D The Travel Show p64	*the*		

UNIT 6 REVIEW p66   **SOUNDS AND SPELLING** voiced and unvoiced consonants (3): /s/ and /z/, /ʃ/ and /ʒ/; /tʃ/ and /dʒ/

LESSON	GRAMMAR/FUNCTION	VOCABULARY	PRONUNCIATION
7 healthy lives BBC VLOGS | Do you eat healthy food?			
7A The little things p68	Present simple: *wh-* questions	Everyday activities (2)	Sentence stress
7B Heroes p70	*was, were*	Common adjectives (3)	Weak and strong forms: *was, were*
7C What's wrong? p72	**How to …** say you're not well	Parts of the body	Word stress
7D Focus on fitness p74	Imperatives	Sports and exercise	

UNIT 7 REVIEW p76   **SOUNDS AND SPELLING** consonants: /b/, /v/, /w/, /l/ and /r/; silent *e* (2): /æ/ to /eɪ/

LESSON	GRAMMAR/FUNCTION	VOCABULARY	PRONUNCIATION
8 time out BBC VLOGS | How was your last holiday?			
8A Weekend break p78	Past simple: regular verbs	Common verbs (2)	*-ed* endings
8B Going out, staying in p80	Past simple: irregular verbs	Free-time activities; time phrases	Silent letters: *didn't*
8C A ticket to … ? p82	**How to …** buy a travel ticket	Transport and tickets	Word stress in prices
8D Kodo drummers p84	*want, would like*		

UNIT 8 REVIEW p86   **SOUNDS AND SPELLING** short and long sounds (2): /æ/, /ɑː/, /ɒ/, /ɔː/, /ə/ and /ɜː/; silent *e* (3): /ɒ/ to /əʊ/

WRITING BANK p90   **GRAMMAR BANK** p108   **VOCABULARY BANK** p133   **COMMUNICATION BANK** p140

READING	LISTENING/VIDEO	SPEAKING	WRITING
Read a text about a good colleague		Talk about people	Write about a good friend; use pronouns
	Understand everyday conversations	Do a quiz and talk about your abilities	
	Understand people making requests and offers	Make requests and offers	
	BBC Street Interviews about birthdays	Talk about your birthday	Write about your birthday
Read an article about lost things		Say where things are	
	Understand people talking about their neighbourhood	Talk about your perfect town	Write a post about your area; use commas
	Understand conversations about finding a place	Ask where a place is	
	BBC Programme *The Travel Show*	Talk about six hours in a city	Describe a city tour
	Understand a podcast about things that make people happy and healthy	Ask about everyday activities	Write an online post; punctuation
Read an article about people's childhood heroes		Ask about famous people **FUTURE SKILLS** Collaboration	
	Understand conversations about not feeling well	Have conversations about health problems	
	BBC Street Interviews about keeping fit	Do a sport and exercise survey	Write a Top Tips post
	Understand someone talking about a weekend break	Talk about past actions	
Read a group chat about people's weekends		Talk about past activities **FUTURE SKILLS** Communication	Write a group chat; linkers: *and*, *but*, *then*
	Understand conversations about buying travel tickets	Ask for travel information	
	BBC Programme *Kodo drummers*	Talk about something you want to try	Complete a questionnaire

SOUNDS AND SPELLING p155 **AUDIOSCRIPTS** p167 **VIDEOSCRIPTS** p173 **VERB TABLE** p175

LEAD-IN

VOCABULARY

international English

1A Match the photos (A–F) with the words in the box.

> a bus   a coffee   a park   a photo
> a pizza   a restaurant

B 🔊 **L.01** | Listen and repeat.

C Work in pairs. Write five more English words that you know.

D Check your ideas in the Vocabulary Bank.

▶ page 124 **VOCABULARY BANK** international words

numbers 0–10

2A Write the words in the box next to the numbers.

> eight   five   four   nine   one   seven
> six   ten   three   two   ~~zero~~

0 zero
1 ....
2 ....
3 ....
4 ....
5 ....
6 ....
7 ....
8 ....
9 ....
10 ....

B 🔊 **L.02** | Listen and check. Then listen again and repeat.

C 🔊 **L.03** | Listen and write the numbers.

D Work in pairs. Student A: Say a number. Student B: Say the next number.

A: Five.
B: Six! … Nine.
A: Ten!

days of the week

3A Number the days in the correct order.

Friday ......
Monday 1
Wednesday ......
Saturday ......
Thursday ......
Sunday ......
Tuesday ......

WEEKLY PLAN						
MON	TUE	WED	THU	FRI	SAT	SUN

B 🔊 **L.04** | Listen and check. Then listen again and repeat.

C Work in pairs. Cover the words in Ex 3A.
1 Say five weekdays.   Monday …
2 Say two weekend days.

classroom language

4A Complete the conversations with the words in the box.

> don't   English   know   page   repeat
> thank   understand   ~~what's~~

Lin: Franco, ¹ what's 'lápiz' in English?
Franco: I don't ² ....
Lin: Jo, what's 'lápiz' in ³ .... ?
Jo: It's a pencil.
Lin: ⁴ .... you!

Jo: It's on ⁵ .... nine.
Stefan: I ⁶ .... understand. Can you ⁷ .... that, please?
Jo: Yes. Page nine. The page in the book. Six, seven, eight, nine …
Stefan: OK, I ⁸ .... Thank you.

B 🔊 **L.05** | Listen and check. Then listen again and say the sentences with the speakers.

C Learn and practise. Go to the Vocabulary Bank.

▶ page 124 **VOCABULARY BANK** classroom language

welcome! 1

VLOGS

Q: Where are you from?

1 Read the question.

2 ▶ Watch the video. How many speakers are from England?

Global Scale of English LEARNING OBJECTIVES

1A LISTENING | Understand people saying 'hello': hello and goodbye

Introduce yourself: present simple *be*: *I, you*; countries and nationalities

Pronunciation: intonation in greetings

Write a chat message to introduce yourself; use capital letters, full stops and question marks

1B READING | Read about people with two jobs: jobs

Pronunciation: word stress in jobs

Talk about people and their jobs: present simple *be*: *he, she, it*

1C HOW TO ... | ask and answer simple questions: the alphabet

Pronunciation: the alphabet

1D BBC STREET INTERVIEWS | Understand street interviews about what's in your bag: common objects

Talk about what's in your bag: singular and plural nouns; *a, an*; *have, has*

Write a lost and found post

Unit 1 | Lesson A

1A Hello

GRAMMAR | present simple *be*: *I, you*
VOCABULARY | hello and goodbye; countries and nationalities
PRONUNCIATION | intonation in greetings

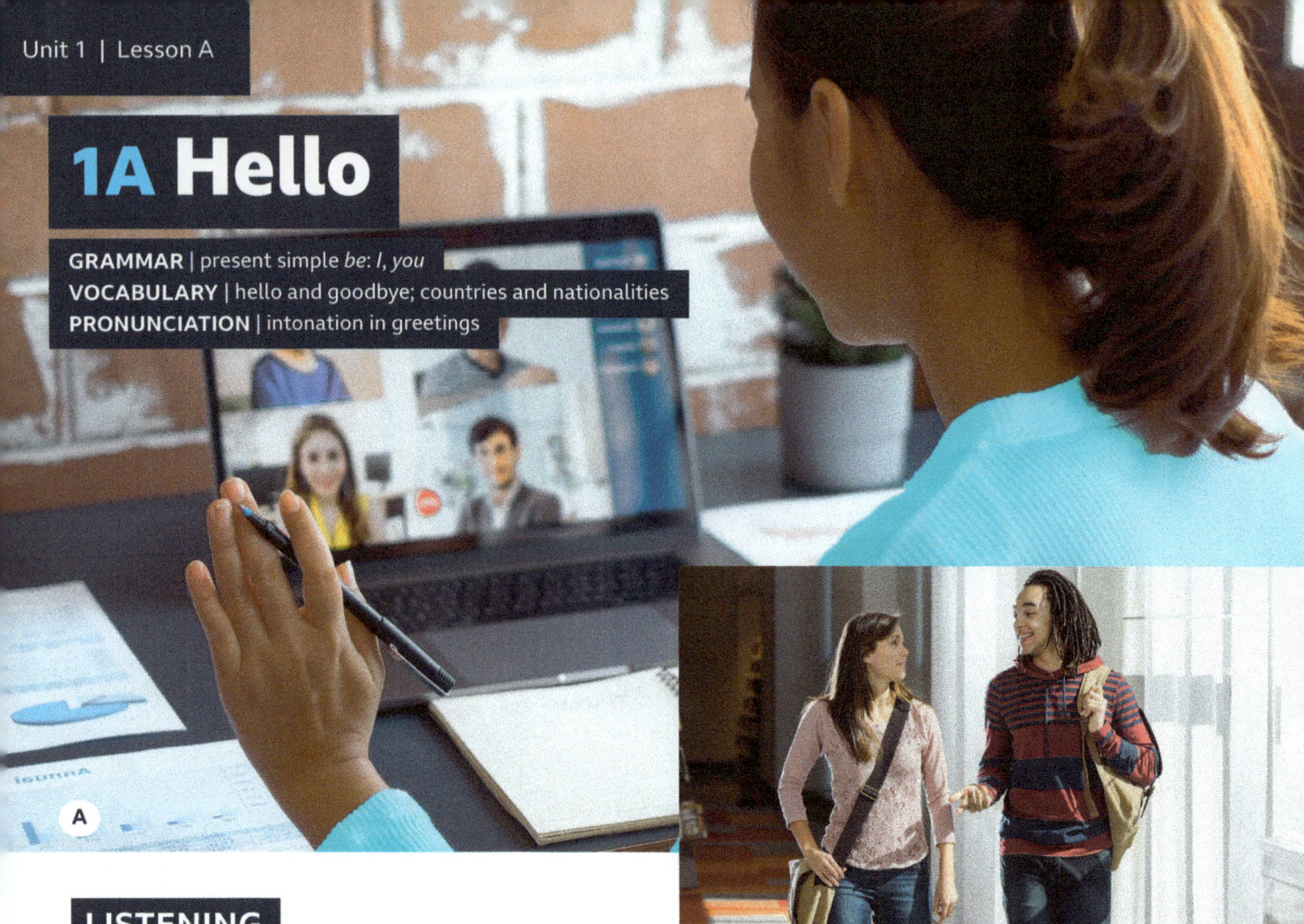

A

B

LISTENING

1 A 🔊 **1.01** | Listen and match the conversations (1 and 2) with the photos (A and B).

B Work in pairs. Match the names with the countries and cities.

name	country	city
James	the UK	Beijing
Sonia	Canada	Toronto
Jack	China	Manchester
		Shanghai
		Vancouver
		London

C 🔊 **1.01** | Listen again and check.

GRAMMAR

present simple *be*: *I, you*

2 A Complete the sentences with *am*, *'m* or *are*.

James: Are you a student?
Sonia: Yes, I am. ¹_____ you?
James: Yes, I ²_____. What's your name?
Sonia: I'm Sonia.
James: I ³_____ James.

B Learn and practise. Go to the Grammar Bank.

▶ page 92 **GRAMMAR BANK**

3 A Complete the conversation.

A: Hello, I ¹ **'m** Shanaya.
B: Hi, Shanaya, ²_____ 'm Ben. Nice to meet you.
A: You too. Where ³_____ you from, Ben?
B: ⁴_____ 'm from Germany.
A: Oh, where in Germany?
B: From Berlin.
A: ⁵_____ you a student here?
B: Yes, I ⁶_____. Are ⁷_____ from the UK, Shanaya?
A: No, I'm ⁸_____. I ⁹_____ from India.

B 🔊 **1.02** | Listen and check.

C Complete the sentence about you.

I'm _____ . I'm from _____ in _____ .
      (first name)   (city)   (country)

D Work in pairs. Say your name, country and town or city. Use Ex 3A to help you.

A: Hello, I'm …
B: Hi, I'm …

VOCABULARY

hello and goodbye

4 Look at the pictures. Complete 1–10 with the greetings in the box.

> Bye   Good afternoon   Goodbye   Good evening
> Good morning   Good night   Hi   ~~Hello~~   Hey   See you

1 Hello
2 ....
3 ....
4 ....
5 ....

6 ....
7 ....
8 ....
9 ....

10 ....

PRONUNCIATION

5 A 🔊 1.03 | **intonation in greetings** | Listen. Match the conversations (1 and 2) with the pictures (A and B).

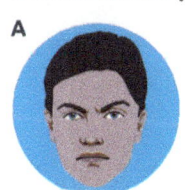 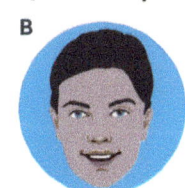
A   B

B Work in pairs. Student A: Say a word or phrase from Ex 4. Student B: Is it picture A or B?

C Work in a different pair. Say hello. Say your name, country, city or town. Then say goodbye. Use friendly intonation.

A: Good morning. I'm Claudia. I'm from Brazil, from Rio de Janeiro.
B: Hello. Nice to meet you. I'm …

SPEAKING

6 Work in pairs and write five countries. Then check your ideas in the Vocabulary Bank.

▶▶ page 125 **VOCABULARY BANK** countries and nationalities

7 A Choose a country and a city from the country.

Japan – Kyoto

B Work in groups and take turns. Guess the city.

A: Where are you from?
B: I'm from Japan.
A: Oh you're Japanese. Are you from Tokyo?
B: No, I'm not.
C: Are you from Osaka?

WRITING

write a chat message to introduce yourself; use capital letters, full stops and question marks

berna2001
Hi, I'm Berna Sadik. I'm Turkish.

Cgarcia2002
Hi, Berna. I'm Carmen. Are you in Turkey now?

8 A Work in pairs and look at the chat messages. Are Berna and Carmen friends?

B Write a chat message to introduce yourself. Go to the Writing Bank.

▶▶ page 88 **WRITING BANK**

Unit 1 | Lesson B

1B Two jobs

GRAMMAR | present simple *be*: *he*, *she*, *it*
VOCABULARY | jobs
PRONUNCIATION | word stress in jobs

VOCABULARY

jobs

1 A Work in pairs and look at the photos (A–D). What are the jobs?

B Match the photos (A–D) with the jobs (1–5). Which job is not in the photos?

1 a doctor
2 a teacher
3 a waiter
4 a taxi driver
5 a singer

PRONUNCIATION

2 A 🔊 1.04 | **word stress in jobs** | Listen and underline the stressed syllable. Then listen and repeat.

a <u>doc</u>tor

B Learn and practise. Go to the Vocabulary Bank.

▶ page 125 **VOCABULARY BANK** jobs

3 Work in pairs. Mime or draw a job. Guess your partner's job.

A: Are you a football player?
B: No, I'm not.
A: Are you a bus driver?
B: Yes, I am.

READING

4 A Read the text. Match the people with the photos in Exercise 1A.

B Complete the table.

name	job in the week	job at the weekend	happy or not?
Carol Harris			
Silvio Rossi			

Weekend work

From Monday to Friday, Carol Harris is 'Doctor Harris'. She's a doctor at a hospital in New York City. 'The job is good, but it's difficult,' she says. 'But the weekend … the weekend is good!' At the weekend she isn't Doctor Harris, she's a singer at a club. 'I'm happy with two jobs,' she says. 'One job in the week and one at the weekend!'

Silvio Rossi is from Rome, Italy. 'I'm a taxi driver here in New York. The job is good and the money is OK,' he says. On Saturday and Sunday, Silvio is a waiter at a restaurant. Is he happy with two jobs? 'Yes, I am. I'm very happy,' he says, 'and New York is a great city.'

D

GRAMMAR

present simple *be*: he, she, it

5 A Underline the verb *be* in the sentences.
1 From Monday to Friday, Carol Harris <u>is</u> 'Doctor Harris'.
2 She's a doctor at a hospital in New York City.
3 At the weekend she isn't Doctor Harris, she's a singer at a club.
4 The job is good.
5 Is he happy with two jobs?

B Complete the rules.
1 For the positive (+), we use *he/she* ¹ is or ²'s .
2 For the negative (-), we use *he/she* ² ....
3 For questions (?), we use ³ .... *he/she*?

C Learn and practise. Go to the Grammar Bank.

▶▶ page 93 **GRAMMAR BANK**

6 A Complete the conversations with the sentences (a–c).
1 A: This is Kevin.
   B: Kevin is a British name. Is he from the UK?
   A: ¹ ....
   B: Is he a friend?
   A: ² ....
   B: Is Busan in China?
   A: ³ ....

a No, it isn't. It's in South Korea.
b Yes, he's a good friend.
c No, he isn't. He's from Busan.

2 A: This is my friend Jane.
   B: Where's she from?
   A: ⁴ ....
   B: Where's Canberra?
   A: ⁵ ....
   B: Is she a student?
   A: ⁶ ....

a No, she isn't. She's a nurse.
b She's from Canberra.
c It's in Australia.

B Work in pairs. Practise the conversations in Ex 6A.

SPEAKING

7 Work in pairs. Practise asking about people. Student A: Go to page 140. Student B: Go to page 143.

8 Work in pairs and take turns. Student A: Show Student B a photo of a friend. Student B: Ask questions.

A: This is Stefan.   B: Is he Polish?

Unit 1 | Lesson C

1C Checking in

HOW TO ... | ask and answer simple questions
VOCABULARY | the alphabet
PRONUNCIATION | the alphabet

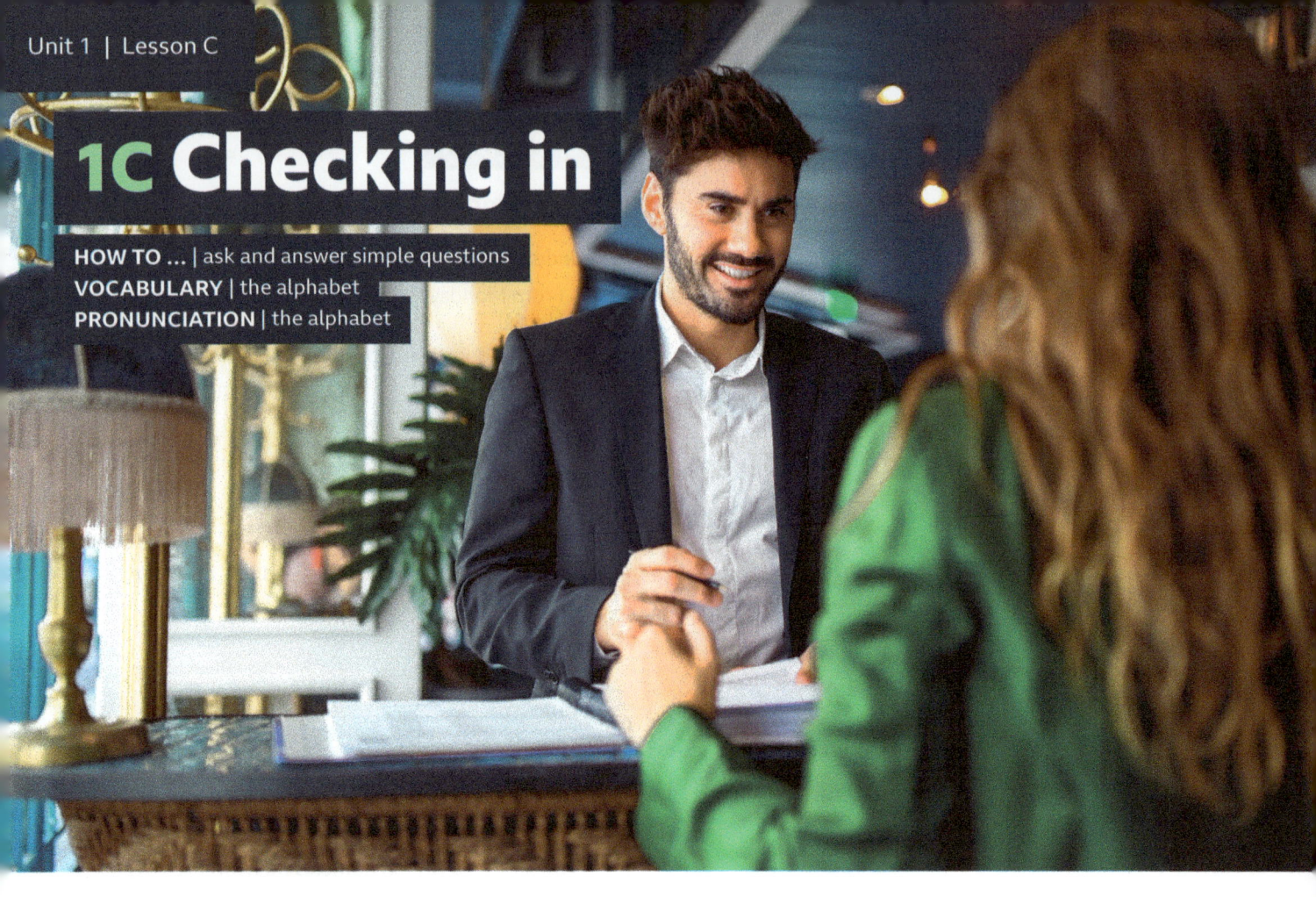

VOCABULARY

the alphabet

1 A Work in pairs. Do you know how to say 1–6?

1 BBC 2 EU 3 OK 4 UK 5 USA 6 www

B 🔊 1.05 | Look at the letters. Listen and repeat.

Aa Bb Cc Dd
Ee Ff Gg Hh
Ii Jj Kk Ll
Mm Nn Oo Pp
Qq Rr Ss Tt
Uu Vv Ww Xx
Yy Zz

PRONUNCIATION

2 A | the alphabet | Complete the table with letters with the same sound.

sound	letter
n**a**me /eɪ/	¹A H _ K
thr**ee** /iː/	²B _ D _ G P _ V
t**e**n /e/	³F L _ N _ X _
n**i**ne /aɪ/	⁴I _
n**o** /əʊ/	⁵O
y**ou** /uː/	⁶Q U _
c**a**r /ɑː/	⁷R

B 🔊 1.06 | Listen and check. Then listen again and repeat.

3 A Work in pairs. Say the letters.

1 ASAP   5 IQ
2 VIP   6 LOL
3 FAQ   7 PS
4 FYI   8 SOS

B Work in pairs. Student A: Go to pages 124–125. Find and spell five words. Student B: Listen and write the words. Student A: Check the spelling.

A: u-n-i-v-e-r-s-i-t-y

How to ...
ask and answer simple questions

4A Look at the pictures (A–C). Find examples of the things in the box.

| first name   surname   address   phone number |

B 🔊 **1.07** | Listen and match the conversations (1–3) with the pictures (A–C).

C 🔊 **1.07** | Listen again. Correct the mistake with a name or a number on each card in Ex 4A.

5A Complete the conversations with the words in the box.

| first name   phone   repeat   spell   surname   ~~what's~~ |

1 A: <u>What's</u> your name?
   B: Imogen Menzie.
2 A: How do you .... your surname?
   B: M-E-N-Z-I-E.
3 A: Great. And what's your .... number?
   B: It's 9-1-3-8-4-5-6-6-0.
   A: Sorry, can you .... that, please?
4 A: What's your .... ?
   B: It's Clarke.
5 A: What's your .... ?
   B: Amelia.

B 🔊 **1.08** | Listen and check.

C Learn and practise. Go to the Grammar Bank.

▶ page 94 **GRAMMAR BANK**

6 Work in pairs. Practise asking and answering simple questions. Student A: Go to page 145. Student B: Go to page 148.

SPEAKING

7A Complete the conversation with the words and phrases.

> Just a moment   Perfect
> Sorry   Thank you
> That's right

Receptionist: ¹ <u>Just a moment</u>. L-O-P-A-Z?
Eduardo: No, L-O-P-E-Z.
Receptionist: ² ...., L-O-P-E-Z?
Eduardo: ³ ....
Receptionist: And your first name ... E-D-U-A-R-D-O?
Eduardo: ⁴ ....
Receptionist: OK, Eduardo. Here's your student card.
Eduardo: ⁵ .... !
Receptionist: No problem.

B Check your answers in Audioscript 1.07 on page 162.

C Read the Future Skills box and do the task.

> **FUTURE SKILLS**
> **Self-management**
> Learn short phrases (e.g. *Perfect! That's right.*) and write them in your notebook. Use three of them in Ex 7D.

D Ask two students for their personal information. Then complete the forms.

First name: ....
Surname: ....
Phone number: ....
City: ....

First name: ....
Surname: ....
Phone number: ....
City: ....

Unit 1 | Lesson D

1D BBC Street Interviews
What's your name?

GRAMMAR | singular and plural nouns; *a, an*; *have, has*
SPEAKING | talk about what's in your bag
WRITING | write a lost and found post

PREVIEW

1 A Work in pairs. Look at the pictures. What's in the bags?

A
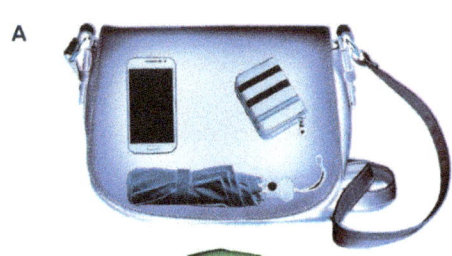

B

B Learn and practise. Go to the Vocabulary Bank.

▶▶ page 126 **VOCABULARY BANK** common objects

Q1: What's your name and how do you spell it?

Q2: What's in your bag?

VIEW

2 A ▶ Watch the first part of the video. Number the speakers in the photos (A–I) in the order you see them.

H 1, A 2

B ▶ Watch again and correct the spelling mistake in four of the names.

1 William   4 Sharon   7 Beba
2 Rachel   5 Ian   8 Lajan
3 Chris   6 Simnit   9 Tom

3 A ▶ Watch the second part of the video. Match the bags in Ex 1A (A and B) with the correct speakers (A–I).

B Work in pairs. Match the sentences with the correct photos (A–I).

1 In my bag I have my phone and my wallet.
2 I have a bottle of water. I have my purse, my keys.
3 I have my laptop and two books.
4 I have an umbrella, my mobile phone and my purse.
5 I have a bottle of water, a notebook and a banana.
6 I have a sandwich in my bag.

C ▶ Watch again and check.

GRAMMAR

singular and plural nouns; *a, an*; *have, has*

4 A Complete the sentences with *a, an, have* or *has*.

1 I have .... umbrella, my mobile phone and my purse.
2 I .... a bottle of water, ... notebook and .... banana.
3 I .... sandwich in my bag.
4 I .... my laptop and two books.
5 Biba .... a phone and a wallet.

B Learn and practise. Go to the Grammar Bank.

▶▶ page 95 **GRAMMAR BANK**

14

1D

SPEAKING

talk about what's in your bag

5 A Make a list of five or more objects in your bag, purse or wallet.

B Read the Key phrases. Which phrases are true for you?

> **KEY PHRASES**
>
> I have five/six things in my bag.
> I don't have a bag, but in my pocket/purse/wallet I have …
> I have a phone, a wallet and my glasses.
> I have two keys/three pens.
> I don't know the name in English.

6 A Work in pairs. Ask and answer the question: *What's in your bag/purse/wallet?* Use the Key phrases to help you. How many things are the same?

B Work in a different pair. Talk about your old partner's bag, purse or wallet.

Luis has a laptop, a phone and …

C Tell the class about one object that you all have.

We all have a photo.

WRITING

write a lost and found post

7 A Match the posts (1 and 2) with the private messages (a and b).

1

LOST
a small black purse. It has a credit card and about €5.
Lost in the High Street today.
Please PM me or phone me on 911 8455.
Thank you!

E   Evi Jannsen   ♡ 2   💬 8   ↪

2

FOUND
a key ring with three keys. Found in Adastra Park this afternoon.
PM me.

J   Jim   ♡ 12   💬 13   ↪

a

 Private message
Hi Jim, you have my keys.

b

 Private message
Hi, Evi, I have your purse. My phone number is …

B Choose one object from your bag. Write a lost post about the object.

C Work in pairs. Look at your partner's post. Write a private message. Say that you have the object.

D Read other students' writing. Match the posts with the private messages.

1 REVIEW

GRAMMAR

1 A Choose the correct alternative.
1 Beijing is in <u>China</u> / Chinese.
2 Mexico City is in **Mexico** / **Mexican**.
3 Lionel Messi is **Argentina** / **Argentinian**.
4 London is in **the UK** / **British**.
5 Scarlett Johansson is **the USA** / **American**.
6 Rome is in **Italy** / **Italian**.

B Write the name of a famous man, a famous woman and a city.

C Work in pairs. Student A: Say a name or a city. Student B: Say the country and nationality.
A: Seoul.
B: Seoul is in South Korea. It's South Korean.

2 A Complete the conversation with the correct form of *be*. Use contractions where possible.
A: ¹_____ you from Australia?
B: Yes, I ² _____ .
A: ³_____ you in France now?
B: No, I ⁴_____ not.

B Work in pairs. Student A: Look at the table and choose a letter (A–P). Student B: Ask questions. Guess the letter.

		in			
		Italy	Brazil	France	Spain
from	Australia	A	B	C	D
	Turkey	E	F	G	H
	Colombia	I	J	K	L
	India	M	N	O	P

B: Are you from India?
A: No, I'm not.
B: Are you from Colombia?
A: Yes, I am.
B: Are you in France?
A: Yes, I am.
B: You're K!

3 A Work in pairs. Choose four words from the box. Write two examples for each word.

> addresses   cities   countries   days   jobs
> letters   names   nationalities

addresses – 32 Main Street, 5 Front Street

B Work in a different pair. Student A: Say your two examples. Student B: Say the correct word from the box.
A: 32 Main Street, 5 Front Street
B: addresses!

VOCABULARY

4 A Write the nationality and the job. Use *a* or *an*.
1 police officer, Colombia a Colombian police officer
2 bus driver, Australia
3 waiter, the UK
4 singer, Poland

B Work in pairs. Student A: Say a job and a country. Student B: Say the nationality and the job. Use *a* or *an*. Then swap roles.
A: nurse, Brazil
B: a Brazilian nurse

5 A Correct the words and phrases. Add the vowels (*a, e, i, o, u*).
1 Gd ftrnn   Good afternoon
2 Hll
3 Gd vnng
4 By
5 Gd mrnng
6 S y
7 Gd nght
8 Gdby

B Put 1, 3, 5 and 7 from Ex 5A in the correct order in the day.

6 A Work in pairs and take turns. Say the words. How do you say the underlined sounds?

J<u>a</u>pan   numb<u>er</u>   bag<u>s</u>
doct<u>or</u>   bus<u>es</u>   ticket<u>s</u>

B Learn and practise. Go to Sounds and Spelling.

▶ page 151 **SOUNDS AND SPELLING**
syllables, stress and /ə/; /s/, /z/, /ɪz/ in plurals

7 A Choose the correct alternative.

English fun facts

The top (number 1) letter in English ¹**is** / **has** 'e'. The top adjective is 'good' and the top noun is 'time'. The top ²**letters** / **words** are 'I' and 'you'.

The English alphabet ³**have** / **has** five vowels: a, e, i, o and u. Greek has seven vowels and the ⁴**Poland** / **Polish** alphabet has nine vowels.

English ⁵**is** / **has** many words from other languages. 'Zero' is from Arabic, 'guitar' is from Spanish and 'shampoo' is from the Indian language Hindi. 'Café' and 'art' are ⁶**in** / **from** French.

English ⁷**number** / **numbers** have difficult spellings! '1' ⁸**is** / **isn't** 'wun', it's 'one'; '2' isn't 'too', it's 'two'; and '8' is 'eight'. Crazy!

B 🔊 R1.01 | Listen and check.

people 2

VLOGS

Q: Where are you now?

1 Read the question.
2 ▶ Watch the video. How many speakers are in Italy now?

Global Scale of English LEARNING OBJECTIVES

2A READING | Read a blog about two people: numbers 11–100; common adjectives (1)
Pronunciation: word stress in numbers
Talk about groups of people: present simple *be*: *we, you, they*

2B LISTENING | Understand someone talking about their family around the world: family; people
Pronunciation: syllables
Talk about your friends and family: possessive adjectives
Write a description of a photo; use *and*

2C HOW TO ... | have short conversations: feelings
Pronunciation: stress in phrases

2D BBC PROGRAMME | Understand a show about a baking competition
Ask about three people: *wh-* questions + *be*
Write a message about a friend

Unit 2 | Lesson A

2A Where are they?

GRAMMAR | present simple be: we, you, they
VOCABULARY | numbers 11–100; common adjectives (1)
PRONUNCIATION | word stress in numbers

VOCABULARY

numbers 11–100

1 A Match the numbers with the words.

18   15
11   19   14
16
13   12
17   20

eleven 11   sixteen
twelve   seventeen
thirteen   eighteen
fourteen   nineteen
fifteen   twenty

B 2.01 | Listen and repeat the numbers in Ex 1A.

C Write the numbers.

30	thirty	70	
40	forty	80	
50	fifty	90	
60		100	a hundred

D 2.02 | Listen and check. Then listen again and repeat.

PRONUNCIATION

2 A 2.03 | word stress in numbers | Listen and underline the stressed syllable.

thir<u>teen</u>   thirty
fourteen   forty
fifteen   fifty
sixteen   sixty
seventeen   seventy
eighteen   eighty
nineteen   ninety

B 2.03 | Listen again and repeat.

C Work in pairs. Student A: Say a number from Ex 2A. Student B: Find the number.

3 A Write the numbers.

1 27 twenty-seven   3 73
2 49   4 56

B Work in pairs and take turns. Say the numbers.

| 67 | 34 | 98 | 52 | 25 | 88 |

C Practise asking and answering simple questions. Student A: Go to page 141. Student B: Go to page 142.

4 A Write the names and ages of three of your friends.

Philip 24   Nick 16   Sally 31

B Work in pairs. Student A: Tell Student B the name of your friend. Student B: Write the name and ask the age.

A: My friend is Philip.
B: How do you spell that?
A: P-H-I-L-I-P.
B: How old is Philip?
A: He's twenty-four years old.

Hi and welcome!

Who are we?

Hi, I'm Francisca. I'm Brazilian, but my home now is in London. I'm 28 and I'm an office worker. My big love is … cycling!

Hello, I'm Finn. I'm from a **small** town (only 180 people!) in Germany and I live in London, too. I'm 32 and I'm a digital designer.

We're married and we're 2OnABikeUK. This is our bike! It's new and it's very good! In the photo, I'm at the front and Francisca is at the back.

Welcome to our blog about bike rides in the UK. One bike ride each month!

2OnABikeUK

MAY: We're in London, by Regent's Canal. The canal is very **old**, about 200 years old. It's nice here, just bikes and people with children or dogs.

JUNE: This month we are in the north of England, in the mountains. They're beautiful. People ask, 'Are you **cold**?' 'No, we aren't, but we're **tired**.'

JULY: This month, hello Wales! We're by the sea. Welsh people are very **friendly**. They ask a lot of questions: 'Where are you from?' 'What's the name of your blog?'

Here we are in the north of England!
A

Regent's Canal in London
B

By the sea in Wales
C

READING

5 A Work in pairs. Look at the photos in the blog (A–C). Which countries are they?

B Read the blog and check your answers.

C Read the blog again. Are the statements True (T) or False (F)?
1 Francisca is married to Finn. T
2 Francisca is from the UK.
3 Finn is from a big city.
4 Finn and Francisca have a bike for two people.
5 The blog is about bike rides around the UK.
6 They're in a different country every week.

D Complete the sentences with the words in bold in the blog.
1 Tom is ninety-eight. He's very ....
2 I'm .... It's only 16 degrees in the classroom.
3 It's 3 a.m. I'm ....
4 Gina says 'hello' to everyone! She's very ....
5 The café only has three tables. It's very ....

E Learn and practise. Go to the Vocabulary Bank.

▶▶ page 127 **VOCABULARY BANK** common adjectives (1)

GRAMMAR

present simple *be*: *we, you, they*

6 A Complete the sentences with the words in the box. Use the blog to help you.

| are   're (x2)   we   aren't |

1 We .... in London, by Regent's Canal.
2 This month .... are in the north of England, in the mountains. They .... beautiful.
3 People ask, '............ you cold?'
4 No, we ....

B Learn and practise. Go to the Grammar Bank.

▶▶ page 96 **GRAMMAR BANK**

SPEAKING

7 Work in pairs. Practise giving information. Student A: Go to page 140. Student B: Go to page 143.

Unit 2 | Lesson B

2B Family and friends

GRAMMAR | possessive adjectives
VOCABULARY | family; people
PRONUNCIATION | syllables

VOCABULARY

family

1 Look at the photos (A–D) and find the people (1–5).
   1 brother and sister
   2 husband and wife
   3 parents and children
   4 father and daughter
   5 mother and son

PRONUNCIATION

2 A | syllables | Do the family words in Ex 1A have one or two syllables?

       2   2
   1 brother and sister (bro-ther, sis-ter)

   B 🔊 2.04 | Listen and check. Then listen again and repeat.

   C Choose the correct word to complete the rule.
   In words with two syllables, the stress is usually on syllable **one** / **two**.

3 Work in pairs. Talk about your family.
   My father is John and my mother is Carol. I have two brothers, Alek and Jeremy.

LISTENING

4 A Work in pairs. Look at the photo of Mark and Mia and answer the questions.
   1 Who do you think is Mark's sister?
   2 Who is his brother?

   B 🔊 2.05 | Listen and check.

   C 🔊 2.05 | Listen again and complete the table.

name	age	country now	job or studies
Mia			a student at school
Jessica		France	has a restaurant
Justin			a writer for a magazine
Emma		the UK	
David	38		

   D Work in pairs and cover the table in Ex 4C. Look at the photos again. What can you remember about the people?
   Mia is eight. She's in Italy. She's a student at school.

20

GRAMMAR

possessive adjectives

5 A Complete the sentences with *my, your, his, her, its, our* or *their*.

1. I have a sister in France, a brother in Colombia and ....our.... parents are in New York.
2. .... sister Jessica and .... husband Thomas are in France.
3. .... son, Justin, is twenty-one.
4. Justin is a writer for a magazine. I don't remember .... name.
5. My brother David and his family are in Colombia. .... wife is Colombian.
6. David says 'Come and visit! It's perfect for .... holiday!'

B Complete the table. Use the sentences in Ex 5A to help you.

subject pronoun	possessive adjective
I	
	its
	your
he	
	her
we	our
	their

C Learn and practise. Go to the Grammar Bank.

▶▶ page 97 **GRAMMAR BANK**

SPEAKING

6 A Work in pairs and answer the question. How many words do you know for people?

woman, friend …

B Learn and practise. Go to the Vocabulary Bank.

▶▶ page 127 **VOCABULARY BANK** people

7 A Work in pairs. Student A: Write questions with *How old*, *Where* and *What* to find the missing information (1–7) in the text. Student B: Go to page 148.

1 How old is Filipa?

Keith McKenny, forty-nine, and Filipa Zampa, ¹............ , (age) are husband and wife. Filipa is ²............ (nationality) and Keith is from the USA. Their home is in ³............ (country), but their children are in Europe. Their daughter Zoe is ⁴............ (age) and she's in Switzerland. She's a ⁵............ (job) in Zurich. Their son Andreas is twenty-three and he's in ⁶............ (country). He's a waiter at a restaurant in ⁷............ (city).

B Ask the questions to complete the text in Ex 7A. Then answer Student B's questions.

8 A Write the names of friends or people in your family.

B Work in pairs. Tell your partner about the people. Ask questions.

WRITING

write a description of a photo; use *and*

9 A Work in pairs. Look at the photo. Where do you think the people are from?

B Read the beginning of the description and check your ideas.

Mei and Ken in the park.

Mei and Ken are friends from Kobe, Japan. Mei is my friend from …

C Write descriptions of your photos. Go to the Writing Bank.

▶▶ page 88 **WRITING BANK**

Unit 2 | Lesson C

2C Small talk

HOW TO ... | have short conversations
VOCABULARY | feelings
PRONUNCIATION | stress in phrases

VOCABULARY

feelings

1 A Work in pairs. Complete the table with the words in the box. They answer the question *How are you?*

> ~~good~~   great   not bad
> really good   not very good

☹	not very well 1 ....
😐	OK 2 ....
🙂	well 3 *good* fine
😊	very well 4 ....
😁	5 ....

B Work in a different pair. Cover the words in Ex 1A. Student A: Ask *How are you?* and point to a face. Student B: Answer the question.

A: How are you?
B: I'm OK. How are you?
A: Not very well.

How to ...

have short conversations

2 A 🔊 **2.06** | Listen and match the conversations (1–3) with the photos (A–C).

B 🔊 **2.06** | Listen again. Match the topics in the box with the conversations (1–3).

> car   children   teacher   work 1

C Complete the conversations.

Dave: Hey, Jen, how ¹ *are* you?
Jen: Hi, Dave. Not bad, thanks. Coffee?
Dave: Yes, ² .... Black ³ .... sugar. ...
       How ⁴ .... work?
Jen: It's OK. How ⁵ .... your children?
Dave: They're great, thanks. ... Oh, look ⁶ .... the time!
       ⁷ .... for the coffee.
Jen: ⁸ .... problem.

Nick: It's a beautiful ⁹ ....
Katie: Yes, it is. How's your new car?
Nick: It's really good. We're very ¹⁰ .... with it.
Katie: Great!
Nick: I'm really hot and tired.
Katie: Me too. Ah, here's my street. See ¹¹ ....
Nick: ¹² .... you later! Say 'hello' to Greg!

Susanna: How's your ¹³ .... teacher? Ms Brown?
Andy: She's really good and she's very ¹⁴ ....

D 🔊 **2.07** | Listen and check.

2C

PRONUNCIATION

3 A | stress in phrases | Match the phrases (1–4) with the stress patterns (a–d).

1 It's a beautiful day.
2 No problem.
3 How's your new car?
4 Me too.

a OOo
b OoOO
c OO
d ooOooO

B 🔊 2.08 | Listen and check.

C Read the Future Skills box and answer the question.

FUTURE SKILLS
Self-management

Have a notebook to write phrases. When you write a phrase, write the stress pattern.
See you later. OoOo.

What are the stress patterns for these phrases?
Thanks for the coffee.
How are the children?

D Learn and practise. Go to the Grammar Bank.

 page 98 **GRAMMAR BANK**

4 A Work in pairs. Use the prompts to make a conversation.

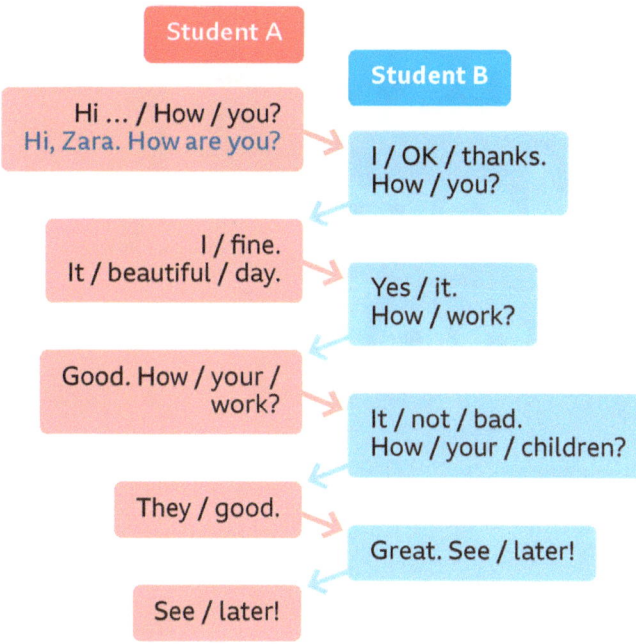

Student A
- Hi … / How / you?
  Hi, Zara. How are you?
- I / fine. It / beautiful / day.
- Good. How / your / work?
- They / good.
- See / later!

Student B
- I / OK / thanks. How / you?
- Yes / it. How / work?
- It / not / bad. How / your / children?
- Great. See / later!

B Practise the conversation.

C Change five things in the conversation. Then practise it again.

Hey, Zara. How are you?

SPEAKING

5 A Complete the *You* column in the table. Use words or pictures from Ex 1A.

	You (A)	Student B	Student C
new job			
new car			
new apartment			
new phone			

B Work in groups of three. Ask about the things in Ex 5A. Complete the rest of the table with pictures or words.

A: How's your new job?
B: It's great! I'm really happy with it. How's your new apartment?
A: It's not bad, but it's very small …

6 Work in pairs. Ask about three of the things in the box. Give real answers.

> work   school   children   parents
> weather in your town   English class

Speak anywhere Go to the interactive speaking practice

Unit 2 | Lesson D

2D BBC Food
Best Home Cook

GRAMMAR: wh- questions + be
SPEAKING: ask about three people
WRITING: a message about a friend

PREVIEW

1 A Work in pairs. Look at the pictures and find:
1 a baker D
2 a birthday cake
3 a competition
4 a judge
5 a presenter
6 a manager
7 a winner

B Read the BBC programme information. Are the sentences (1–3) true (T) or false (F)?
1 *Best Home Cook* is a competition.
2 Five men and five women are in the competition this week.
3 The programme information has the names of the three winners.

BBC: Best Home Cook

Best Home Cook is a competition to find the best home baker. The people in the competition aren't bakers – they have other jobs. Today is week four, and seven bakers are in the competition. The task is to make a children's birthday cake. Who are the three winners this week?

VIEW

2 A Go to page 150 and discuss the birthday cakes.

B ▶ Watch the BBC video clip. Who are the three winners?

C ▶ Work in pairs. Match the names (1–6) with the information (a–f). Then watch again and check.
1 Robin c
2 Suzie
3 Georgia
4 Oli
5 Katie
6 Elisabetta

a is a model
b is fifty-two
c is from Bristol
d is from Northern Ireland
e is a restaurant manager
f is thirty-three

D ▶ Watch the BBC video clip again and choose the words and phrases you hear.
1 This is **Good/Best** Home Cook.
2 Our presenter is **Claudia/Clara** Winkleman.
3 Suzie is **33/36**.
4 Oli is **34/44** and he's married.
5 Elisabetta is from **Spain/Italy**, but now her home is in London.
6 Sarah's 42 and has a son. They're from **Manchester/Liverpool**.

2D

BBC

GRAMMAR

wh- questions + be

3 A Complete the questions for the sentences in Ex 2D. Write *Who, What, Where* or *How*.

1 .... is the name of the programme?
2 .... is the presenter?
3 .... old is Suzie?
4 .... old is Oli?
5 .... is Elisabetta from?
6 .... are Sarah and her son from?

B Learn and practise. Go to the Grammar Bank.

▶▶ page 99 **GRAMMAR BANK**

SPEAKING

ask about three people

4 A Write the names of three people.
- someone in your family • a friend • someone from work or school

B Work in pairs. Tell each other two or three things about each person.

Adriana is a good friend. She's from Romania. She's 33 years old.

C 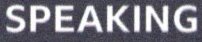 **2.09** | Listen to a woman answer questions about her three people. Match the names (1–3) with who they are (a–c).

1 Judi   a someone from work
2 Dennis   b a friend
3 Kenji   c a brother or sister

D 🔊 **2.09** | Listen again and tick the Key phrases you hear.

KEY PHRASES

Who's Judi?   Is he married?
Where's she from?   He has a wife and two sons.
She has a good job in a shop. Kenji is someone from work.
He's a good friend.   What's his job?
How old is he?   He's really nice.

5 Work with another partner. Ask and answer questions about your three people in Ex 4A. Use the Key phrases to help you.

WRITING

write a message about a friend

6 A Read the message from Sonia. Choose the correct alternative.

1 Martina is **her friend/someone in her family**.
2 She's **British/Argentinian**.
3 **Sonia/Martina** is in Manchester.

Hi Jen,

How are you and the family? I'm really well.

My friend Martina is in Manchester now. She's a good friend from university. She's from Argentina and she has a job with an Argentinian TV company. She's really nice and very friendly.

Can I give Martina your phone number? She's in Manchester for two weeks.

Sonia xxx

B Work in pairs. Write a message to your partner about one of your three people in Ex 4A.

25

2 REVIEW

GRAMMAR

1 Complete the conversation with the words in the box.

> 're   are (x2)   aren't (x2)   her   his
> my   their   what   where   who

A: ¹.......... are they?
B: They're ².......... friends.
A: ³.......... are ⁴.......... names?
B: ⁵.......... name's Mira and ⁶.......... name's Abdul.
A: ⁷.......... you friends from university?
B: No, we ⁸.......... . We're friends from work.
A: ⁹.......... are they from?
B: They ¹⁰.......... from Canada.
A: ¹¹.......... they married?
B: No, they ¹².......... . They're brother and sister.

VOCABULARY

2 A Write the answers. Use words.

1 Thirty-seven + five =   forty-two
2 Seventy-five - fifteen = ...
3 Twenty-two + sixteen = ...
4 Ninety-two - fifty-two = ...

(+ plus, - minus)

B Complete the questions with a number.

1 What's 11 + ...?
2 What's 48 - ....?
3 What's 16 + ...?
4 What's 90 - ....?

C Work in pairs. Ask and answer the questions in Ex 2B.

3 A Complete the adjectives with vowels (a, e, i, o, u).

1 b_g   8 fr__ndly
2 h_t   9 t_r_d
3 n_w   10 b_d
4 y__ng   11 sm_ll
5 g__d   12 c_ld
6 b___t_f_l   13 _ld
7 f_v__r_t_   14 gr__t

B Work in groups and play a memory game. Cover the words in Ex 3A. Student A: Say the number of letters and the first letter. Other students: Say the adjective.

A: It has four letters. The first letter is 'g'.
B: Good!

C Take turns to say a sentence. Use one of the adjectives from Ex 3A.

Good morning. Jack's a **good** student. My phone is very **good**.

4 A Look at the picture of a family. Who says the sentences (1–4)?

1 My mother is Di. Guy or Hena
2 My son is Ed.
3 My husband is Andy.
4 My daughter is Hena.

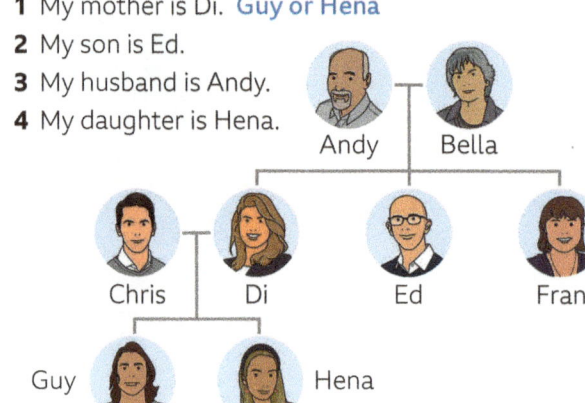

B Write three more sentences about the people in Ex 4A. Use sentences 1–4 to help you.

C Work in pairs. Student A: Say one of your sentences. Student B: Say the name of the person.

5 A Work in pairs and take turns. Say the words. How do you say the underlined sounds?

s<u>i</u>x   wh<u>e</u>re
s<u>i</u>xt<u>ee</u>n   <u>wh</u>at
good aftern<u>oo</u>n <u>wh</u>o

B Learn and practise. Go to Sounds and Spelling.

▶ page 152 **SOUNDS AND SPELLING** short and long sounds (1): /ɪ/, /iː/, /ʊ/, /uː/; /w/ and /h/ in question words

6 A Choose the correct alternative.

A family business

Burger24/7 is a hamburger restaurant in Adelaide, Australia. Tom, the manager, says, 'We're all family here. ¹**My / Your** mother is here from 10 o'clock in the morning. My son and daughter ²**is / are** at school, but ³**their / they're** in the restaurant at weekends.'

Tom's wife ⁴**is / are** also in the family business. She's Samantha, and she's the head chef. 'People ask us, "⁵**Why / Where** are you open 24/7?"' says Samantha. 'Well, ⁶**we're / our** open 24/7 because people are hungry 24/7.'

Samantha has a brother, but he's not in the family business. 'He says we're crazy. He asks me, "Samantha, ⁷**what / who** are your summer holiday plans?"' Samantha says, 'What holiday? ⁸**We're / Our** restaurant is our life!'

B ▶ R2.01 | Listen and check.

things 3

VLOGS

Q: What's your favourite thing?

1 Read the question.

2 ▶ Watch the video. How many speakers say their bike?

LEARNING OBJECTIVES
Global Scale of English

3A READING | Read a blog about people's favourite things: things; colours

Talk about people's things: possessive *'s*

Pronunciation: possessive *'s*

Write about favourite things; use *and*, *but*

3B LISTENING | Understand a radio phone-in about people's desks: desk objects

Pronunciation: sentence stress

Talk about your desk: present simple *have* + *yes/no* questions (*I*, *you*, *we*, *they*)

3C HOW TO … | shop for clothes: clothes

Pronunciation: intonation

3D BBC STREET INTERVIEWS | Understand street interviews about people's shopping habits: shops

Ask and answer questions about buying online and in shops: likes, dislikes and opinions

Write a personal profile

Unit 3 | Lesson A

3A Favourites

GRAMMAR | possessive 's
VOCABULARY | things; colours
PRONUNCIATION | possessive 's

VOCABULARY

things

1 A Work in pairs. Match the photos (A–H) with the words in the box.

> bed   bike   camera   car
> coffee machine   guitar   ring   watch

B Work in pairs. Look at the photos in Ex 1A. Say the number of things you have.

I have three of the things.

C Guess the things your partner has.

A: I think you have a car.
B: That's right. I have a Kia.

2 Work in pairs. What colour are the things in the photos in Ex 1A? Check your ideas in the Vocabulary Bank.

▶ page 128 **VOCABULARY BANK** colours

READING

3 A Read the text about favourite things. Which things have information about 1–4?

1 colour   car   3 age
2 country or nationality   4 family

B Work in pairs. Student A: Close your book. Student B: Read one sentence from the text, but don't say the thing. Student A: Say the name of the thing.

A: It's old and Spanish.
B: The guitar.

What's your favourite thing?

 Will Reese ♥ 12 💬 13

My favourite thing is my car. It's blue and it isn't very big, but I love it. It's perfect for the town!

 A

 Grace Sneed ♥ 10 💬 13

My camera. It's my father's camera, but I have it in my apartment. It's from Germany. It's old but very good for black and white photos.

 B

 Pat Lambert ♥ 12 💬 9

My favourite thing is my guitar. It's beautiful. It's old and Spanish.

 C

 Naomi Emmett ♥ 15 💬 14

My bed. It's good when I'm tired. It's good when I'm happy or sad. It's my perfect place. I love it!

 D

3A

GRAMMAR

possessive 's

4 A Correct the sentences. Add 's. Use the text in Ex 3A to help you.
1 It's my father camera.
2 My favourite thing is my grandmother ring.
3 The watch is Swiss and it has my mother name, Alice, on it.

B Work in pairs. Complete the rule.

We use person + ... for the possessive.

C Learn and practise. Go to the Grammar Bank.

▶▶ page 100 **GRAMMAR BANK**

Monique Beck
♥ 13 💬 12 ↪

My favourite thing is my grandmother's ring. It's about a hundred years old and it's from her mother. It's beautiful and I love it!

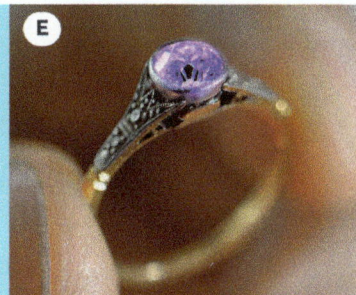

Theo Olsen
♥ 13 💬 10 ↪

It's my coffee machine. I have two big cups of coffee in the morning – perfect cups of coffee from my Italian coffee machine.

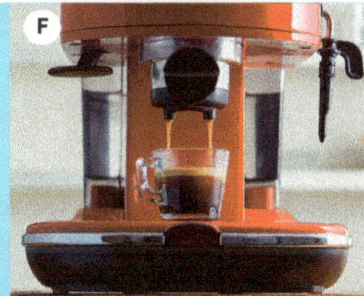

David Fox
♥ 14 💬 16 ↪

My favourite thing is my bike. I don't have a car. My bike is green, my favourite colour, and it's very important to me.

Alicia Porta
♥ 11 💬 11 ↪

My watch is really important to me. It's Swiss and it has my mother's name, Alice, on it. She has a new watch now, but I love her old watch.

PRONUNCIATION

5 A 🔊 3.01 | possessive 's | Listen to the sentences. Match the words in bold in (1–4) with the sounds: /s/, /z/ and /ɪz/.
1 my **grandmother's** ring   /s/
2 **Pat's** guitar   /z/ grandmother's
3 **Alice's** watch.   /ɪz/
4 my **father's** camera

B Work in pairs. Read the sentences. What is the sound in bold in each sentence: /s/, /z/ or /ɪz/?
1 Susan**'s** bag   4 Irmak**'s** guitar
2 Philip**'s** phone   5 Darsh**'s** bike
3 Felix**'s** camera   6 Carol**'s** book

C 🔊 3.02 | Listen and check.

D Work in pairs. Student A: Say a thing in one of the photos (A–H). Student B: Say the person and their thing.

A: Coffee machine.
B: It's Theo's coffee machine.

SPEAKING

6 Work in pairs. Practise asking about pictures. Student A: Go to page 144. Student B: Go to page 147.

WRITING

write about favourite things; use and, but

7 A Work in pairs. Complete the sentences with *and* or *but*. What are the sentences about? Check your answers in the text in Ex 3A.
1 It's blue and it isn't very big, ... I love it.
2 It's about a hundred years old .... it's from her mother.

B Write an online comment about your favourite things. Go to the Writing Bank.

▶▶ page 89 **WRITING BANK**

8 A Choose 3–5 of your favourite things. Make notes about them.

My phone - new, from my parents, important to me

B Work in groups. Talk about your things. Use your notes to help you.

9 📷 Bring a photo of a favourite thing to the next lesson. Prepare to talk about it.

Unit 3 | Lesson B

3B What's on your desk?

GRAMMAR | present simple *have* + yes/no questions (*I, you, we, they*)
VOCABULARY | desk objects
PRONUNCIATION | sentence stress

VOCABULARY

desk objects

1 A Work in pairs. Look at the photo. Which objects are NOT on your desk or table at home?

B Work in pairs. Look at the photo again. Which objects in the box are in the photo?

> bottle of water   book   computer   cup of coffee
> glasses   headphones   keyboard   mouse
> notebook   pen   pencil   phone   plant
> scissors   sticky notes   tablet

C Work in pairs. Student A: Choose three objects from the photo and say the first letter. Student B: Guess the objects.

A: P
B: Plant?
A: No …

D Work in pairs. Close your books. Write ten objects you remember from the photo.

LISTENING

2 A 🔊 **3.03** | Listen to two people talking about their desks. Who talks about the desk in the photo, Sandy or Joe?

B 🔊 **3.03** | Listen again. Tick the objects that Sandy and Joe have on their desks.

	Sandy	Joe
computer	✓	
keyboard		
mouse		
notebook		
pen		
pencil		
sticky notes		
glasses		
headphones		
plant		

GRAMMAR

present simple *have* + *yes*/*no* questions (*I, you, we, they*)

3A Choose the correct alternative.

1 I **have** / **has** a computer and a keyboard.
2 I **have** / **I'm have** a cup of coffee.
3 I **no have** / **don't have** any pencils on my desk.
4 Joe, do you **has** / **have** a job?
5 Yes, I **does** / **do**.
6 **Do you have** / **Have you** a photo of your son?
7 No, I **don't** / **don't have**.
8 I **have** / **do have** two notebooks.

B 🔊 3.04 | Listen and check.

C Learn and practise. Go to the Grammar Bank.

▶▶ page 101 **GRAMMAR BANK**

PRONUNCIATION

4A 🔊 3.05 | sentence stress | Underline the two or three stressed words in each sentence. Then listen and check.

1 A: Do you <u>have</u> a <u>job</u>?
   B: Yes, I do.
2 A: Do you have a photo of your son?
   B: No, I don't.

B 🔊 3.05 | Listen again. Choose the correct pronunciation of *Do* in the questions in Ex 4A.

/də/ / /duː/

C 🔊 3.05 | Listen again and repeat.

5A Work in pairs. Underline the main stressed words in the questions. Then take turns to say the questions. Pay attention to word stress and the pronunciation of *Do*.

1 Do you <u>have</u> a <u>camera</u>?
2 Do you have any headphones with you?
4 Do you have any plants in your room?
5 Do you have a favourite coffee cup?
6 Do you have a favourite pen?

B Work in a different pair. Ask and answer the questions in Ex 5A.

A: Do you have a camera?
B: No, I don't, but I have a camera on my phone.

SPEAKING

6A Read the Future Skills box and do the task.

> **FUTURE SKILLS**
> **Collaboration**
>
> Sometimes you don't understand – that's normal! Use short phrases to check (e.g. *Sorry? Can you repeat that? I don't understand*.). Use two of these phrases in Ex 6B.

B Work in pairs. Practise asking about objects. Student A: Go to page 144. Student B: Go to page 147.

7 Work in pairs. Tell your partner about your desk or workspace. What's different about the things on your desk? What's the same?

We both have pens, sticky notes …

Unit 3 | Lesson C

3C How much is it?

HOW TO ... | shop for clothes
VOCABULARY | clothes
PRONUNCIATION | intonation

A

VOCABULARY

clothes

1 A Work in pairs. Look at the photos (A–C) and answer the questions.

1. Match the photos with the types of shopping: in a market, online and in shops.
2. Which is your favourite type of shopping: in a market, online or in shops? Why?
3. Do you have any big markets in your town/city?
4. Are they for clothes, food or something different?

B Look at the photos again. Which clothes in the list are in the photos?

- a light green shirt
- white jeans
- a blue jacket
- a light brown jacket
- a dark blue coat
- a white T-shirt

C Learn and practise. Go to the Vocabulary Bank.

⏩ page 129 **VOCABULARY BANK** clothes

B

C

How to ...
shop for clothes

2 A 🔊 **3.06** | Listen to two conversations. Match the conversations (1 and 2) with the correct photos (A–C).

B Listen again. Tick the clothes that you hear.

C 🔊 **3.06** | Listen again. What are the prices?

3 A Work in pairs. Complete the conversations with the words in the box.

| is   excuse   ~~how~~   much   size   try |

1 Ian: _How_ much is it?
   Becca: I don't know. _____ me?
   Man: Can I help you?
   Becca: Yes, how _____ is this jacket? ...
           Can I _____ it on?
   Man: Yes, of course.

2 Nia: What _____ are you? Medium?
   Ryan: No, large. ...
           Is it dark blue?
   Nia: Yes, it is.
   Ryan: Then blue. How much _____ it?

B 🔊 **3.07** | Listen and check.

C Learn and practise. Go to the Grammar Bank.
▶ page 102 **GRAMMAR BANK**

PRONUNCIATION

4 A 🔊 **3.08** | intonation | Listen and match the sentences (a and b) with the pictures (1 and 2). Which sounds friendly, 1 or 2?

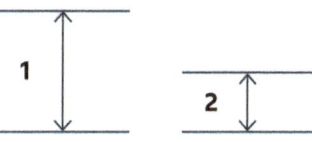

1 a Excuse me. 1
  b Excuse me.
2 a How much is this jacket?
  b How much is this jacket?
3 a Can I try it on?
  b Can I try it on?

B 🔊 **3.08** | Listen again and repeat.

SPEAKING

5 A Work in pairs. Look at the prompts for a conversation in a shop. Use the prompts to make the questions (1–5).

B Practise saying the questions. Remember to sound friendly and use a wide voice range.

C Roleplay the conversation.

D Swap roles and change the words in bold.

6 Work in pairs. Practise shopping conversations. Student A: Go to page 145. Student B: Go to page 148.

Unit 3 | Lesson D

3D BBC Street Interviews
Shopping

GRAMMAR | likes, dislikes and opinions
SPEAKING | ask and answer questions
WRITING | write a personal profile

Holly

Vincent

Rachael

PREVIEW

1 A Work in pairs and discuss the questions.
  1 Where do you shop?
  2 What do you buy in shops?
  3 What do you buy online?

B What shops do you know?

C Check your ideas. Go to the Vocabulary Bank.

▶▶ page 130 **VOCABULARY BANK** shops

Q1: What do you buy online?
Q2: What shops do you like?

VIEW

2 A ▶ Watch the first part of the video. How many speakers buy food online?

B Work in pairs. What do you remember? Complete the sentences.
  1 Elijah: I buy things for the h............ online.
  2 Joe: Online I buy v............ games and in shops I buy food.
  3 Josh: Online I buy c............ and in shops I also buy food.
  4 Nic: I buy c............ food online. I buy clothes in shops.
  5 Kirsty: I buy books online and I buy s............ in the shop.
  6 Vincent: I buy t............ online.

C ▶ Watch again and check.

3 A ▶ Watch the second part of the video. Are the statements True (T) or False (F)?
  1 Six speakers talk about clothes shops.
  2 Two speakers talk about video game shops.

B ▶ Watch again. Which shops in the box do the speakers talk about?

baker's   bookshops   butcher's   cafés
clothes shops   pet shops   sports shops

GRAMMAR

likes, dislikes and opinions

4 A Look at the words in bold. Which are positive 😊 and which are negative ☹?
  1 I **love** clothes shops, I **hate** butchers and I love cafés.
  2 I **like** sports shops, and I **dislike** clothes shops.
  3 I **like** clothes shops. I **don't like** bookshops.

B Choose the correct alternative.
  1 I **think** / **like** computer shops are great.
  2 I **hate** / **think** food shops are OK.

C Learn and practise. Go to the Grammar Bank.

▶▶ page 103 **GRAMMAR BANK**

SPEAKING

ask and answer questions

5 A Read the question prompts and the answers. Which answers are true for you?

1 Favourite type of shop? chocolate shop
2 Favourite time of the day? evening
3 Favourite actor/actress? Timothée Chalamet
4 Favourite singer? Billie Eilish
5 Three favourite colours? black, yellow, pink
6 Two favourite apps? BBC, maps
7 Favourite city? Paris
8 Tennis or football? tennis
9 Electric cars or bikes? electric cars
10 E-books or books? books
11 Cats or dogs? cats
12 Hot or cold weather? cold weather

B Work in pairs. Match the question phrases (a–d) with the question prompts (1–12) in Ex 5A.

a What's your … ?
b What are your … ?
c Who's your … ?
d Do you like … ?

1 a What's your favourite type of shop?

C Work in a different pair. Ask and answer the questions in Ex 5B. Use the Key phrases to help you.

KEY PHRASES

I like food shops/sports shops.
I love Paris. I think it's really beautiful.
I really like tennis.
I like football a lot.
I think electric bikes are/Billie Eilish is great.
Me too.
I don't.
I don't like cats.

D Tell the class about two things that you and your partner like.

We both like Adele and we think football is great.

WRITING

write a personal profile

6 A Read the personal profile. Match the information that Alysha gives with 1–12 in Ex 5A.

GlobalAllTogether

Hi everybody!

I'm Alysha and I'm from Germany. I'm a college student in Sweden. I like cold weather, so Sweden is perfect for me.

I love films, and my favourite actress is Zendaya. She's in the *Spider-Man* films.

I like sports, but I don't like football. Tennis is my favourite sport.

Now tell me about you!

Alysha

I like cold weather – 12

B Choose three questions from Ex 5A. Write your personal profile. Give information about yourself and answer the three questions.

C Swap profiles. Who likes the same things as you?

3 REVIEW

GRAMMAR

1 A Complete the sentences. Use possessive 's.

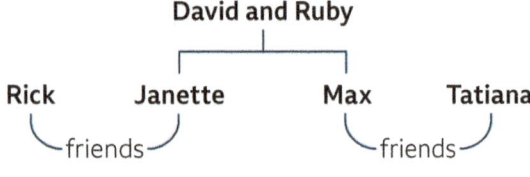

David and Ruby
Rick — Janette — Max — Tatiana
(Rick & Janette: friends; Max & Tatiana: friends)

1 Ruby is _David's_ wife.
2 Janette is _____ sister.
3 David is _____ husband.
4 Rick is _____ friend.
5 Max is _____ brother.
6 Tatiana is _____ friend.

B Write the names of six people (family or friends). Work in pairs. Ask questions about the people.

A: Who's Hesna?
B: She's my brother's friend.

2 A Use the prompts to make questions.

1 you / have / bike?
   Do you have a bike?
2 you / have / email address?
3 they / have / British friends?
4 we / have / Italian speaker / in the office?
5 Ramin and Vineeta / have / apartment?
6 you / have / cat?

B Complete the short answers. Then match the answers (a–f) with the questions (1–6) in Ex 2A.

a Yes, I _do_. It's black and it's really friendly. 6
b No, they _____ – they have a beautiful house.
c Yes, we _____. Violetta is Italian.
d No, they _____. Their friends are all American.
e No, I _____, but I have a small car.
f Yes, I _____. It's IanXY24@skymail.com

3 A Add the words in brackets to the sentences.

1 I love hotels. (really)
   I really love hotels.
2 I hate supermarkets. (really)
3 I like big cities. (a lot)
4 I think the internet is great. (really)
5 I think phones are bad. (really)
6 I like red cars. (a lot)

B Change the sentences in Ex 3A so they are true for you.

C Work in pairs and ask questions. Use the sentences in Ex 3A. How many things do you have in common?

A: Do you love hotels?
B: No, I don't. I hate hotels.
A: Me too.

VOCABULARY

4 A Find six colours, six objects and six types of clothes.

P	U	R	P	L	E	W	A	T	C	H
B	X	J	O	M	J	P	I	N	K	E
L	B	E	R	E	S	W	T	Z	E	A
A	L	A	A	S	B	H	R	I	Y	D
C	L	N	N	K	I	I	O	M	B	P
K	H	S	G	I	R	T	U	O	O	H
W	C	R	E	R	T	E	S	B	A	O
V	O	H	O	T	E	D	E	N	R	N
T	A	B	L	E	T	V	R	R	D	E
F	T	S	S	C	I	S	S	O	R	S
S	U	I	T	G	L	A	S	S	E	S
B	R	O	W	N	A	D	R	E	S	S

B Write seven objects and types of clothes that you have. Add their colours. Make two items false.

purple jeans

C Work in pairs. Student A: Say your sentences. Student B: Guess the false sentences.

A: I have some purple jeans.
B: False!
A: No, it's true!
B: Really? Do you have a photo?

5 A Work in pairs and take turns. Say the words. How do you say the underlined sounds?

pencil   car   tablet
bed   guitar   dark

B Learn and practise. Go to Sounds and Spelling.

> page 153 **SOUNDS AND SPELLING**
> voiced and unvoiced consonants (1): /p/ and /b/, /k/ and /g/, /t/ and /d/; sounds at the end of words

6 A Complete the words (1–10) with vowels (a, e, i, o, u).

A blogger's bag

I have a travel blog and every weekend I go to a new city. It's important for me to travel with a very small bag! I have extra clothes – two ¹sh_rts, a ²j_mp_r for cold evenings and a ³j_ck_t for rain. I don't have my ⁴l_pt_p – I love it, but it's really big, so I have a ⁵n_t_b__k and a pen. It's my favourite pen – a present from my parents. And I have ⁶st_cky n_t_s in different colours – ⁷y_ll_w for information about food, ⁸bl__ for hotels and ⁹gr__n for transport. And I have a phone with a great ¹⁰c_m_r_. That's it!

B R3.01 | Listen and check.

every day 4

VLOGS

Q: What's your favourite meal of the day – breakfast, lunch or dinner?

1 Read the question.

2 ▶ Watch the video. How many speakers say 'breakfast'?

Global Scale of English — LEARNING OBJECTIVES

4A LISTENING | Understand people from different countries talking about lunch: food and drink
Talk about food: adverbs of frequency
Pronunciation: word stress
Write an email to a friend

4B READING | Read about an influencer's daily routine: everyday activities (1); telling the time
Ask and answer about your daily routine: present simple: regular verbs (*he*, *she*, *it*)
Pronunciation: third person -s

4C HOW TO … | order in a café: café words
Pronunciation: intonation in *or* phrases

4D BBC PROGRAMME | Understand a documentary about three people around the world
Ask about someone's routine: present simple: yes/no questions (*he*, *she*, *it*)
Write a quiz

Unit 4 | Lesson A

4A Time for lunch!

GRAMMAR | adverbs of frequency
VOCABULARY | food and drink
PRONUNCIATION | word stress

VOCABULARY

food and drink

1 Work in pairs. Which types of food in the box are in the photos (A–C)?

> apple   banana   chicken   egg
> fish   mushroom   pasta   rice
> sandwich   steak   tomato

PRONUNCIATION

2 A 🔊 4.01 | **word stress** | Work in pairs. Match the words in Ex 1 with the syllable patterns (1–3). Then listen and check.

1 O   egg
2 Oo   apple
3 oOo

B 🔊 4.01 | Listen again and repeat.

C Learn and practise. Go to the Vocabulary Bank.

▶▶ page 131 **VOCABULARY BANK**
food and drink

LISTENING

3 A Work in pairs and discuss the questions.

1 In the week, do you have a small lunch or a big lunch?
2 What do you have for lunch every day?

B 🔊 4.02 | Listen and number the photos (A–C) in the order you hear about them.

C Look at the table. Tick the food you remember from the conversations in Ex 3B.

	Isabel	Miki	Aiden		Isabel	Miki	Aiden
 🍝	✓			 🐟			
 🍚		✓		 🍗			
 🍅				 🍏			
 🥪			✓	 🥚			
 🧀				 ☕			

D 🔊 4.02 | Listen again and check.

38

GRAMMAR

adverbs of frequency

4A Put the adverbs in bold in the correct place on the line.

1 We **usually** have lunch together.
2 I **never** drink coffee. I hate it.
3 After lunch I **always** drink tea, green tea, every day.
4 I **sometimes** eat my sandwich at my desk or I sometimes go to the park.
5 We **often** eat fruit, an apple or a banana.

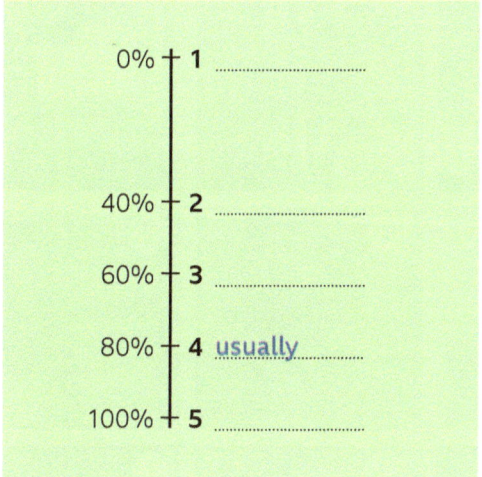

0% — 1 ....
40% — 2 ....
60% — 3 ....
80% — 4 usually
100% — 5 ....

B Learn and practise. Go to the Grammar Bank.

▶▶ page 104 **GRAMMAR BANK**

5A Put the words in the correct order to make sentences.

1 fruit. / eat / I / often
   I often eat fruit.
2 eat / I / home. / don't / at / often
3 have / vegetables / dinner. / sometimes / I / for
4 I / birthday. / eat / always / on / steak / my
5 drink / with / I / tea / usually / milk.
6 never / eat / chicken. / I
7 lunch. / always / coffee / I / have / after
8 for / eggs / never / I / breakfast. / eat

B Work in pairs. Which sentences are true for you? Change the other sentences to make them true.

SPEAKING

6A Complete the box with food and drink items. Use your own ideas.

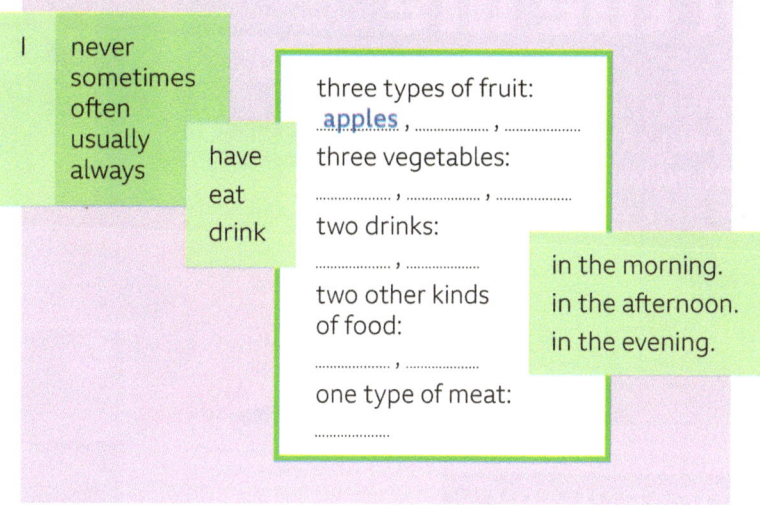

I
never
sometimes
often
usually
always

have
eat
drink

three types of fruit:
apples , ... , ...
three vegetables:
.... , ... , ...
two drinks:
.... , ...
two other kinds of food:
.... , ...
one type of meat:
....

in the morning.
in the afternoon.
in the evening.

B Work in pairs. Tell your partner five things about your eating habits.

A: I often eat chicken in the evening.
B: Really? Me too. I never drink milk in the morning.

C Work in a different pair. Close your books. Tell your partner three more things.

7 📷 Bring a photo of your lunch to the next lesson. Prepare to talk about the photo.

WRITING

write an email to a friend

8A Read the email and answer the questions.

1 What is Stacy's news?
2 What are her questions?
3 What are your answers to her questions?

Hi Jade,

How are you? We're all well and we have lots of news. Pete has a new job in the city. Susie has a new apartment!

We're really happy about your visit next weekend. I have two questions about food. 1. What do you like for breakfast? 2. Do you eat meat and fish?

See you soon,

Stacy x

B Write an email to a friend. Go to the Writing Bank.

▶▶ page 89 **WRITING BANK**

Unit 4 | Lesson B

4B A day in the life

GRAMMAR | present simple: regular verbs (*he, she, it*)
VOCABULARY | everyday activities (1); telling the time
PRONUNCIATION | third person *-s*

VOCABULARY

everyday activities (1)

1 A Work in pairs. Match the pictures (A–I) with the phrases in the box. Which phrase is not in the pictures?

> finish work   get home   ~~get up~~   go to bed
> go to work   have lunch   leave home
> make dinner   start work   watch TV

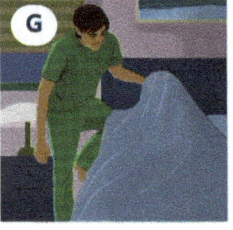  

B Complete the sentences with the phrases in Ex 1A.

1 I ...*get up*... at 6 a.m. and have breakfast.
2 I .... at about 8 a.m.
3 I .... by bus.
4 I .... at 9.
5 I .... at about 1 p.m.
6 I .... at 5 p.m.
7 I .... at 6.
8 I .... at 7 and we eat together.
9 After dinner, we ....
10 I .... at 11.

C Change the sentences in Ex 1B so they are true for you. Then work in pairs and compare your answers.

A: I get up at seven. What about you?
B: I get up at six.

D Learn and practise. Go to the Vocabulary Bank.

▶ page 132 **VOCABULARY BANK**
telling the time

2 Work in a different pair. Ask and answer questions about your daily routines. Use the phrases in Ex 1A to help you.

A: What time do you get up?
B: Monday to Friday I get up at half past seven. At the weekend I get up at nine.

READING

3 A Look at the photos of MelseyPop and answer the questions. Then read the text and check your answers.

1 What's her job?
2 How old is she?
3 Is she happy in her job?

B Read the text again. Are the statements True (T) or False (F)?

1 'I get up at seven o'clock.' F
2 'I have breakfast with my family.'
3 'I work alone in the morning.'
4 'I make videos about different things.'
5 'Two of my friends are YouTubers.'
6 'I don't have dinner.'
7 'I watch videos in the evening.'

C Work in pairs and look at the text again. Find two things that are the same and two things that are different about your day.

GRAMMAR

present simple: regular verbs (*he, she, it*)

4A Work in pairs. Underline the verbs.
1 Nineteen-year-old MP <u>gets up</u> at six.
2 'Tom loves my videos.'
3 She goes to a café.
4 She finishes her video.
5 She doesn't have breakfast.

B Complete the rules for regular verbs. Use Ex 3A to help you.
1 For the positive we use *she/he* + infinitive + ...*s*.... .
2 With verbs ending -*o* and -*sh* we use *she/he* + infinitive + ...
3 For the negative we use *she/he* .... + infinitive.

C Look at the text again. Find eight more examples of *he, she* + the present simple.

D Learn and practise. Go to the Grammar Bank.
▶ page 105 GRAMMAR BANK

PRONUNCIATION

5A 🔊 4.03 | third person -*s* | Listen and write the verbs.

B 🔊 4.03 | What is the sound of the verb ending? Write /s/, /z/ or /ɪz/ for each verb in Ex 4A. Then listen again and repeat.

makes – /s/

C Work in pairs. Cover the text in Ex 2A. Use the verbs in Ex 4A to talk about MP's day.

A: MP makes videos about her life.

SPEAKING

6A Talk to other students. Ask questions and complete the table.

	gets up at eight.
	goes on social media before breakfast.
	has breakfast in a café.
	doesn't drink coffee.
	makes sandwiches for lunch.
	doesn't work or study in the evening.
	watches YouTube or Instagram videos every day.
	listens to the news every day.

A: Do you get up at eight, Fatima?
B: No, I don't.
A: Do you get up at eight, Abdul?
C: Yes, I do.

B Work in pairs. What information about other students is the same for you?

A: Abdul gets up at eight, but I get up at 7.30.
B: I get up at 7.30, too. Fatima goes on social media before breakfast. I go on social media before breakfast, too.
A: Me too.

A day in the life: a YouTuber

YouTuber MelseyPop – 'MP' is her nickname – talks about her day.

Nineteen-year-old YouTuber MP gets up at six and checks her emails and messages. 'I usually go on social media for about twenty minutes in the morning.' She doesn't have breakfast, only a big cup of coffee. She starts work at seven. MP makes videos about her everyday life: her clothes, her favourite music, food, football, her family, everything! At twelve she goes to a café and has lunch with two friends. 'They make YouTube videos too, and we watch our videos together.'

After lunch, MP gets home at about two and she finishes her video. In the afternoon, she often does something new in her videos – for example she makes something new for dinner.

'I always have dinner with my family. They're important to me – my parents and my brother, Tom. Tom loves my videos! He thinks they're great.' In the evening she usually writes ideas for new videos, or she listens to music.

'I go to bed at 10.30 or 11. That's my day and I love it!'

4C Can I have … ?

HOW TO … | order in a café
VOCABULARY | café words
PRONUNCIATION | intonation in *or* phrases

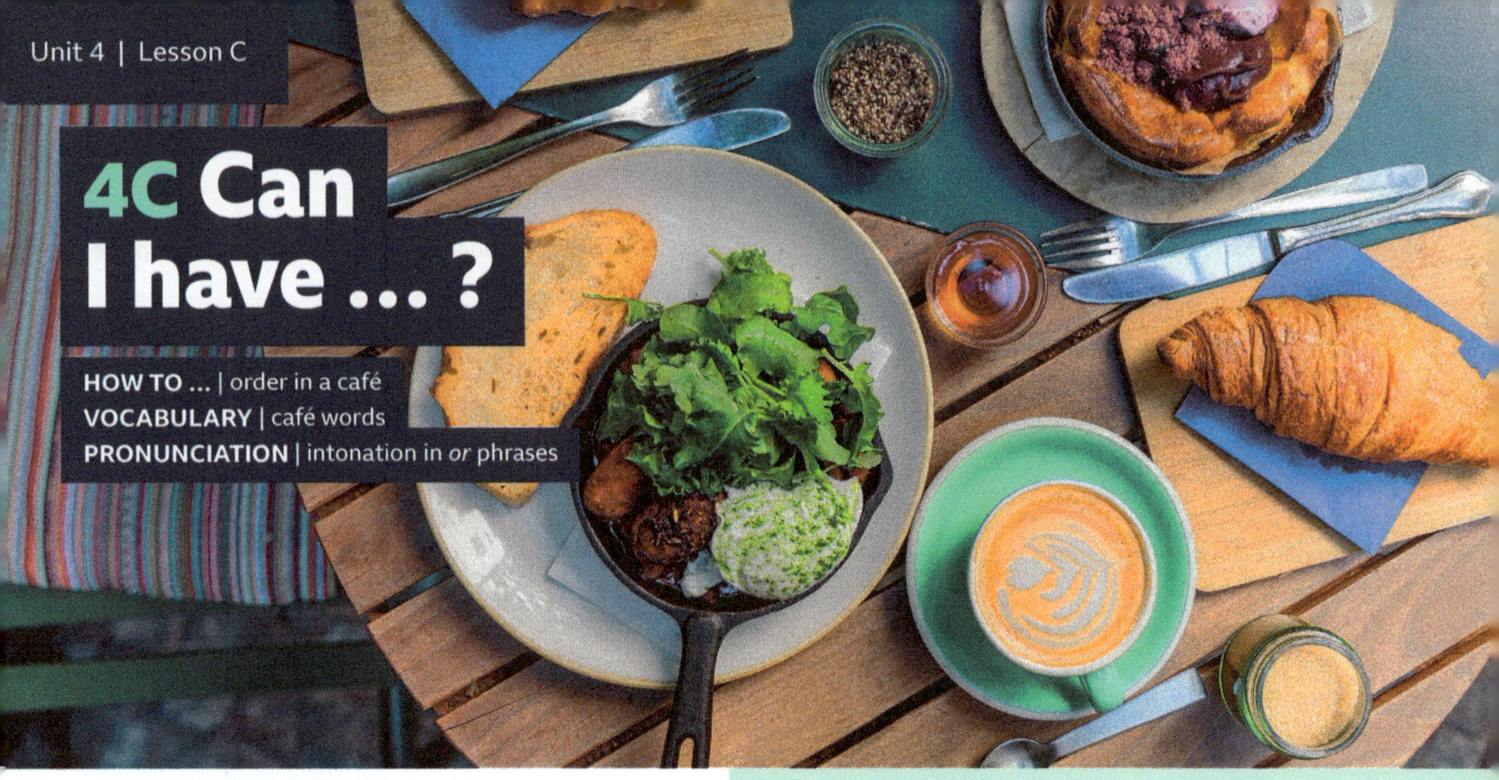

VOCABULARY

café words

1 A Work in pairs. Look at the photo above and discuss the questions.

1 Do you like the food in the photo?
2 Do you often go to cafés?
3 When do you go, in the morning or afternoon?
4 What's your favourite café?
5 What do you eat and drink there?

B Which things in the box are in the photo?

cup	fork	pastry	salt	sugar	toast

C Learn and practise. Go to the Vocabulary Bank.

page 132 **VOCABULARY BANK** café words

2 A Match the phrases (1–8) with the pictures (A–H) in the menu.

1 eggs and toast with a coffee or a tea
2 tea
3 coffee: latte, espresso or Americano
4 a sandwich and a coffee or a tea
5 a fruit juice
6 a pastry and a coffee or a tea
7 toast and a coffee or a tea
8 a mineral water

B Work in pairs and look at the menu again. Student A: Order some food and drink. Student B: Answer and point to the correct picture.

A: A pastry and a coffee, please.
B: Here you are.

Breakfast Specials
A
+ or = £4.80
B
+ or = £5.50
C
+ or = £5.50
D
+ or = £4.50
Drinks
E
or or = £3.00
F
£2.50
G
orange or apple
£2.50
H
still or sparkling
£2.00

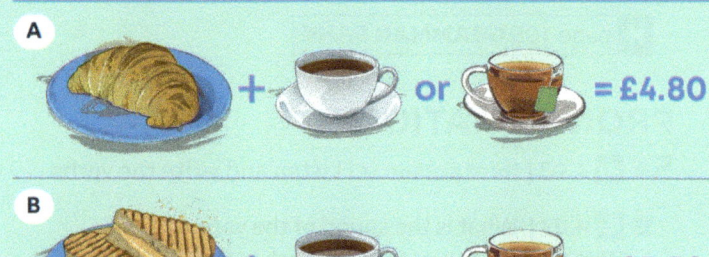

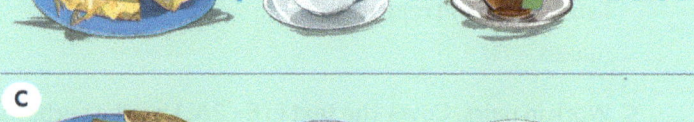

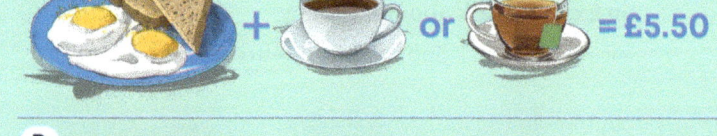

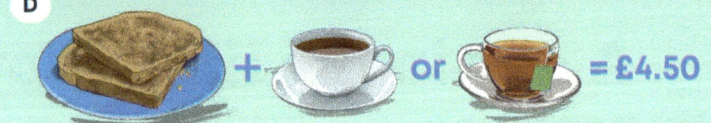

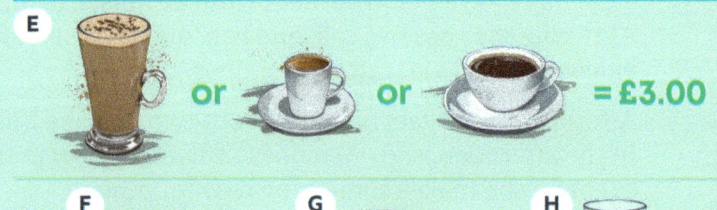

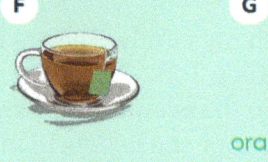

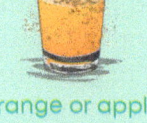

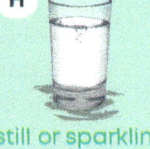

How to ...
order in a café

3 A 🔊 **4.04** | Look at the menu again and listen to three conversations. Match the conversations (1–3) with the food and drink (A–H).

B Read the conversations and choose the correct alternative.

W: ¹**Can I / I can** help you?
C: Yes. Can I have a coffee, ²**please / thanks**?

W: OK, a coffee with milk. Here ³**I / you** go.
C: ⁴**What / How** much is that?
W: ⁵**Is / That's** three pounds.

C: Can I have a tea and a pastry, please?
W: Yes, just a ⁶**moment / time**. Here you ⁷**have / are**.

W: ⁸**Anything / Everything** else?
C: No, ⁹**thank / thanks** you.

W: Coffee ¹⁰**and / or** tea?
C: Coffee, please.

W: Still or sparkling?
C: Oh, sparkling, please. How much is ¹¹**that / he**?
W: Just a moment. Let me ¹²**check / watch**.

C 🔊 **4.05** | Listen and check.

4 A Complete the table.

¹ .... I have	a tea,	please?
Coffee	²	tea?
Still		sparkling?
Sparkling,		³ ....

B Learn and practise. Go to the Grammar Bank.

▶ page 106 **GRAMMAR BANK**

PRONUNCIATION

5 A 🔊 **4.06** | intonation in *or* phrases | Listen. Which intonation do you hear, 1 or 2? Then listen again and repeat.

1 Coffee or tea?   2 Coffee or tea?

B Work in pairs. Ask and answer questions. Use the words in the box.

> apple/orange?   still/sparkling?
> espresso/latte?

A: Can I have a fruit juice, please?
B: Apple or orange?
A: Orange, please.

SPEAKING

6 A Work in pairs. Student A: Look at the café menu. You are the customer. Order food and drink. Student B: Go to page 145.

MENU

☕ $4.10

☕ $3.40

🍶 $2.70

🍩 $4.40

🥪 $5.40

B: Can I help you?
A: Yes, can I have a cup of coffee, please?
B: Espresso, latte or Americano?

B The waiter brings the food and drink. Now ask for two of the things in the pictures (A–D).

A 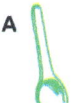   B   C    D

C Swap roles. Go to page 145.

Unit 4 | Lesson D

4D BBC Documentary
Earth From Space

GRAMMAR | present simple: *yes/no* questions (*he, she, it*)
SPEAKING | ask about someone's routine
WRITING | write a quiz

PREVIEW

1 A Work in pairs. Do you have a favourite animal? What is it?

B Read the BBC programme information and answer the questions.
 1 Where is each photo (A–C)?
 2 Who are the people in the photos?

Earth From Space

From space we can see colours and shapes, water and land. Zoom in and we can see many different lives. Thousands of parakeets eat at the home of Joseph Sekar in the middle of a big city in India. A fire lookout named Billy Ellis stands on a tower in the mountains of Colorado in the USA. And in a village in Peru a young girl, Elvira, meets her favourite animal, a manatee, for the first time.

VIEW

2 A Work in pairs. Match the words in the box with the parts of the programme (1–3).

> breakfast   forest   lake   rice   rivers   steps

 1 Joseph Sekar and the parakeets
 2 Billy Ellis, the fire lookout
 3 Elvira and the manatee

B ▶ Watch the BBC video clip and check your ideas.

C ▶ Complete the sentences with the correct form of the verbs in the box. Then watch again and check.

> come   get up   live   ~~make~~   say   see   watch

 1 He gets up at half past five every morning and <u>makes</u> rice for the parakeets.
 2 Four thousand parakeets .... to his home every day.
 3 I ...., have a cup of coffee and then I'm ready to go.
 4 Billy is a fire lookout. He .... the forest for fires.
 5 No, not often, but when he .... a fire, it's his job to call the firefighters.
 6 Manatees usually .... in rivers.
 7 Elvira watches the manatee and .... goodbye.

D Work in pairs and answer the questions.
 1 Which story do you like best?
 2 Do you have forest fires in your country?
 3 Which animal do you like best: the parakeets or the manatee? Why?

GRAMMAR

present simple: yes/no questions (*he*, *she*, *it*)

3 A Work in pairs. Choose the correct question form (a, b or c).

  a He sees many forest fires?
  b Does he see many forest fires?
  c Is he see many forest fires?

B Learn and practise. Go to the Grammar Bank.

▶ page 107 GRAMMAR BANK

SPEAKING

ask about someone's routine

4 A Work in pairs and read the conversation. Who are the speakers talking about, Joseph, Billy or Elvira?

A: Does this person get up early?
B: I don't know.
A: Does he or she have a job?
B: No.
A: Does he or she like animals?
B: Yes.

B 🔊 4.07 | Look at the photos on page 125 and listen to the conversation. Which job is it?

C 🔊 4.07 | Listen again and tick the Key phrases you hear.

> **KEY PHRASES**
> OK, ask me questions.
> Let me see. OK, is it a man or a woman?
> Does she drive in her job?
> Yes, she does.
> Does she wear special clothes in her job?
> So, who is it?
> You're right.
> You're wrong. Guess again.
> Now it's my turn.

5 Work in pairs. Student A: Choose a person on page 10 or page 125. Student B: Ask questions and guess the job. Use these questions and the Key phrases to help you.

Does he/she work:
- indoors/outdoors/at home?
- in an office/a school/a hospital?
- in the day/in the evening/at night/from 9 a.m. to 5 p.m./at the weekend?
- with computers/with other people/alone?

Does he/she:
- make things?
- travel?
- wear special clothes?

WRITING

write a quiz

6 A Work in pairs. Read the quiz questions and choose the correct answers (a–c).

> ### Quiz: Earth From Space
> **1 Does Joseph Sekar live in:**
>   a the USA?
>   b India?
>   c Pakistan?
>
> **2 Does he get up at:**
>   a five o'clock?
>   b half past five?
>   c six o'clock?
>
> **3 Does he say:**
>   a he loves animals?
>   b he loves all living things?
>   c all living things are important?

B Check your answers in the videoscript on page 173.

C Work in pairs. Write a quiz about Billy Ellis and Elvira. Use the videoscript to help you.

D Swap questions with another pair.

4 REVIEW

GRAMMAR

1 A Put the adverbs of frequency (a–f) in order (1–6).

- a always
- b never   1
- c not often
- d often
- e sometimes
- f usually

B Make the sentences true for you. Add an adverb of frequency.

1 I go to a café for lunch.
2 I eat toast for breakfast.
3 I have pastries in the morning.
4 I use chopsticks.
5 I drink tea from a glass.
6 I read a newspaper online.
7 I listen to music in English.
8 I go to bed after midnight.

C Work in pairs and compare your answers. Write your partner's answers.

D Work in a different pair. Tell your new partner about your old partner. How many things are the same?

A: Cindy sometimes goes to a café for lunch.
B: Me too!
A: Really? I always have lunch at home.

2 A Make a note of these things.

1 three apps on your phone
2 three places in your town (supermarket, clothes shop, etc.)
3 the name of a friend, and one thing your friend eats, drinks, watches

B Work in pairs. Ask questions about one of the topics (1–3) from Ex 2A. Use *Does*.

1 Does your phone have …
2 Does your town have …
3 Does your friend eat …

VOCABULARY

3 A Correct the food and café words. Add one letter.

1 bef beef   2 mushoom   3 sal   4 nife
5 chiken   6 ornge   7 peper   8 frk
9 met   10 bred   11 sugr   12 poon

B Complete the table with three food words in each column. Look at page 131 for more ideas.

I like	I don't like	I never eat

C Work in pairs. Student A: Say one of your food words. Student B: Guess which column the food word is in.

A: Chicken.
B: You like it.
A: Yes!

4 A Complete the word webs.

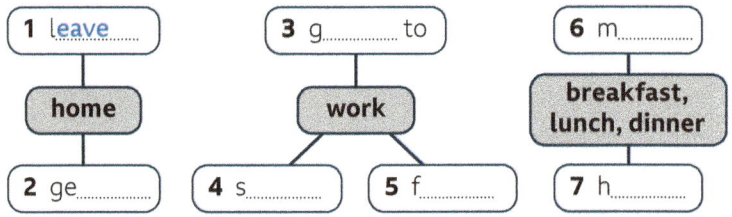

B Work in pairs. Student A: Say three phrases from Ex 4A. Student B: Say the phrases in the order that you do them.

A: have dinner, make breakfast, go to work
B: make breakfast, go to work, have dinner

5 A Work in pairs and take turns. Say the words. How do you say the underlined sounds?

apple   napkin   lunch   money   breakfast
red   Does he understand?   Yes, he does.

B Learn and practise. Go to Sounds and Spelling.

▶ page 154 **SOUNDS AND SPELLING**
short vowels: /e/, /æ/, /ʌ/; does: /dʌz/ or /dəz/?

6 A Complete the words in the text.

What do you eat?

I eat five times every day, not really five meals, sometimes it's just a snack. In the morning at six, I have a ¹ban___ and some chocolate and then I have training. For breakfast I always have five ²eg__ and some ³fru__. At ⁴h___ past ten, I have breakfast number two, but nothing big, for example a ⁵b___ of ⁶cer___ with milk. I sometimes have a ⁷sandw___ for lunch, or I have ⁸pas__. Dinner is usually at ⁹quar___ to seven. I often have a ¹⁰ste__ with ¹¹ri__, ¹²che___ and two or three ¹³vegetab___, maybe a ¹⁴pot___, some ¹⁵carr___ and some ¹⁶tomat___. I love ice cream, but I never eat it – not before a race!

B 🔊 R4.01 | Listen and check.

WRITING BANK

1A write a chat message to introduce yourself

berna2001 — Hi, I'm **Berna** Sadik. I'm **Turkish**.

Cgarcia2002 — Hi, Berna, **I**'m Carmen. Are you in Turkey now?

berna2001 — No, I'm not. I'm in **London**. **Where** are you from?

Cgarcia2002 — I'm from Madrid in **Spain**.

1 A Read the chat. Match the rules (1–6) with the words in bold.

We use capital letters for:
1 the first word in a sentence.
2 *I*.
3 the name of a person.
4 a city.
5 a country.
6 a nationality.

B Choose the correct words to complete the rules.
1 We use a full stop (.) **at the end / in the middle** of a sentence.
2 We use a question mark (?) at the end of a **sentence / question**.

C Correct eleven mistakes in the chat with capital letters and five mistakes with full stops or question marks.

hi, i'm martín

where are you from

i'm from mexico

are you american

yes, but i'm in australia now

2 A Work in pairs. Write a chat message to your partner.
Hi, I'm …

B Swap messages. Reply to the message.

2B write a description of a photo; use *and*

Mei and Ken in the park

Mei and Ken are friends from Kobe, Japan. Mei is my friend from university. She's a teacher and her husband Ken is a businessman. They have two children, a daughter and a son, aged one and three. Their names are Sora and Aya. They're a lovely family and we often have video calls with them.

1 A Look at the photo and read the description. What are the people's names?

B Correct the sentences. Add *and*. Then check your answers in the text in Ex 1A.

      and
1 Mei/Ken are friends from Kobe, Japan.
2 She's a teacher her husband Ken is a businessman.
3 They have two children, a daughter a son …

C Read the text in Ex 1A again. Find four more examples of *and*.

2 A Look at the photo of your friends. Complete the notes.

Names ……………
Where are they in the photo? ……………
Nationalities ……………
Jobs or studies ……………
Family relationships (*son*, *daughter*, etc.) ……………

B Write a description of the photo. Use your notes in Ex 2A. Add more information. Use *and* three or four times.

C Swap descriptions with other students. Are they different from your description?

3 Write descriptions of three more photos. Bring them to the next lesson.

WRITING BANK

3A write about favourite things; use *and*, *but*

1 A Read the rule. Then match 1–3 with a–c to make sentences. Use *and* or *but*.

+ ... + or - ... - use *and*
+ ... - or - ... + use *but*

1 She has a new watch now,
2 My bike is green
3 It's old and my room is cold,

and
but

a my bed is my favourite place.
b I love her old watch.
c it's very important to me.

B Choose the correct option (a or b) to complete the sentences.

1 My favourite chair isn't beautiful, but
  a I love it.   b it's in my bedroom.
2 My favourite colour is red and
  a my bike is blue.   b my favourite day is Monday.
3 We have five dogs and
  a three cats.   b we don't have a garden.
4 I'm from Mexico, but
  a now I'm in Colombia.   b my parents are in Mexico City.
5 English is great, but
  a it's difficult.   b it's easy.

C Complete the sentences with your own ideas.

1 My .... is very old, but …
2 My .... is new and …
3 I have a beautiful .... and …
4 My .... has .... , but …

My guitar is very old, but it's very good.

D Work in groups. One student: Read one of your sentences from Ex 1C. Other students: Ask questions.

How old is it?
What colour is it?
Where is it from?

2 A Read the description and answer the questions in Ex 1D.

One of my favourite things is my rug. It's from Morocco and it's very old, about 100 years old. It's orange, blue and red. It has a hole in it, but it's really beautiful and I love it.

B Choose one favourite thing and write about it. Use the text in Ex 2A to help you.

4A write an email to a friend

Hi Jade,

How are you? We're all well and we have lots of news. Pete has a new job in the city. Susie has a new apartment!

We're really happy about your visit next weekend. I have two questions about food. 1. What do you like for breakfast? 2. Do you eat meat and fish?

See you soon,

Stacy x

1 A Read the email from Stacy again. Then look at the sentences (a–h) from Jade's reply. Put them in the correct order.

a It's great news about Pete and Susie.
b You ask about breakfast.
c See you on Saturday,
  Jade xxx
d And yes, I eat meat, but I don't like fish.
e Hello Stacy,
  I'm very well, thanks.
f I don't often eat a big breakfast, but cereal or toast is good and I love coffee.
g What's Pete's new job, and where's Susie's new apartment?

B Read sentences a–g again and find Jade's answers to Stacy's questions.

C Look at your answers to Ex 1A. Put the topics (a–c) in the correct order.

a Answer the questions about the visit.
b Answer the question *How are you?*
c Say something about the person's news.

D Complete the table with the phrases in the box.

Hi Jeff   See you soon   Love
Hey Paola   Speak soon   Hello Ed

starting an email	
finishing an email	

2 Write a reply to Stacy's email. Use your answers from Ex 1C to help you.

GRAMMAR BANK

1A present simple *be*: *I, you*

REFERENCE ⏪ page 8

Use *be* in the present simple to say your name, your country and your age.
I'm Nadia. **I'm** from Argentina. **I'm** seven.
We use *be* with a subject pronoun.
I'm from Canada. NOT ~~Am from Canada.~~

Positive (+)

subject	be	phrase
I	'm	Ottavia.
	am	nine.
You	're	a student.
	are	from the UK.

We use **'** for a missing letter.
I ~~a~~m → I'm   You ~~a~~re → You're

We use contractions (*I'm, you're*) in speaking and in emails and messages to friends.
I'm Tracy. **You're** a teacher.

Negative (-)

subject	be + not	phrase
I	'm not	John.
	am not	in Paris.
You	aren't	from Spain.
	are not	American.

We use a contraction (*aren't*) in speaking and in emails and messages to friends. You **aren't** in Italy.
We can also say *You're not*. **You're not** American.

Yes/No questions

You **are** a student.   **Are you** a student?

be	subject	phrase
Am	I	in class A1?
Are	you	OK?

Short answers

Yes/No	subject	be
Yes,	I	am.
No,		'm not.
Yes,	you	are.
No,		aren't.

We don't use contractions with short answers with *yes*.
Yes, I **am**. NOT ~~Yes, I'm.~~   Yes, you **are**. NOT ~~Yes, you're.~~
We can also say No, **you're not**.

Wh- questions with *Where*

Where	be	subject
Where	am	I?
	are	you from?

PRACTICE

1 Complete the conversation with the words in the box.

| am   are (x2)   I (x2)   ~~'m~~   not   you |

A: Hello, I ¹ _'m_ Sue.
B: Hi, ² .... 'm Tony.
A: ³ .... you from the USA?
B: No, I'm ⁴ ....
A: Where ⁵ .... you from?
B: I'm from Canada. And you? Are ⁶ .... from Australia?
A: Yes, I ⁷ ....
B: Where in Australia?
A: ⁸ .... 'm from Brisbane.
B: Nice to meet you.
A: And you.

2 Change five verbs (*am, are*) to contractions (*'m, 're*) in each conversation.

1 A: Hi Gavin, how are you?

   B: Hey Leah. ~~I am~~ well, thanks. Where are you?
   A: I am in South Africa.
   B: Really! You are in South Africa! Where in South Africa?
   A: I am in Cape Town today and in Johannesburg tomorrow. Are you well?
   B: Yes, I am. And you?
   A: I am very well, thank you.

2 A: Hello. Are you a teacher?
   B: No, I am not.
   A: OK, you are a student.
   B: Yes, I am. I am Elif Buruk.
   A: Where are you from, Elif?
   B: I am from Turkey.
   A: OK. You are in class A1.

GRAMMAR BANK

1B present simple *be*: *he*, *she*, *it*

REFERENCE ⏪ page 11

We use *be* in the present simple with jobs, nationalities and prices.

He's a teacher. She's Colombian. It's four dollars.

We use *be* with a subject pronoun.

It's six euros. NOT ~~Is six euros.~~

Positive (+)

subject	be	phrase
He	's	British.
She	is	a doctor.
It		ten pounds.

We use **'** for a missing letter.

He ~~is~~ → He's   She ~~is~~ → She's   It ~~is~~ → It's

We use contractions (*he's, she's, it's*) in speaking and in emails and messages to friends.

He's Indian. She's in Tokyo.

Negative (-)

subject	be + not	phrase
He	isn't	in class.
She	is not	a nurse.
It		from Brazil.

We use contractions (*he/she/it isn't*) in speaking and in emails and messages to friends. **He isn't in London. Sylvia isn't American.**

We can also say *He's not, She's not, It's not*. **He's not from China.**

Yes/No questions

It is hot.  Is it hot?

be	subject	phrase
Is	Mike	OK?
	Greta	from Germany?

Short answers

Yes/No	subject	be (+ not)
Yes,	he	is.
No,	she	isn't.

We don't use contractions with short answers with *yes*.

Yes, he is. NOT ~~Yes, he's.~~

We can also say *No, she's not*.

Wh- questions

Wh- question word	be	subject
Where	's	the airport?
What	is	'olá' in English?

PRACTICE

1 Choose the correct alternative.
1 He / <u>She</u> 's a businesswoman.
2 **It's** / **She's** a city in Mexico.
3 **Is** / **He's** French.
4 Montaz **isn't** / **no is** from Brazil.
5 **Imani is** / **Is Imani** Vietnamese?
6 **What's** / **What** your name?
7 Is my class A1? Yes, **it's** / **it is**.
8 A: Is Benita a police officer?
   B: No, **she's not** / **she not**.
9 Rashid **no is** / **isn't** in Istanbul.
10 **What's** / **Where's** Jordan from?

2 Use the prompts to make answers.
1 Where's Madrid?
   It / Spain. **It's in Spain.**
2 Where's Ho Chi Minh City?
   It / Vietnam.
3 Where's Ariana Grande from?
   She / the USA.
4 Where's Son Heung-min from?
   He / South Korea.
5 Is Agnieszka Holland from Poland?
   Yes / she.
6 Is Naomi Osaka from South Africa?
   No / she.
7 Is Nicole Kidman from the UK?
   No / she. She / Australian.
8 Is Bogotá in Brazil?
   No / it. It / Colombia.
9 Is John Boyega American?
   No / he. / He / the UK.

3 Complete the questions.
1 **Where's** Emma?
   She's in London.
2 .... Venice .... Spain?
   No, it isn't. It's in Italy.
3 .... Oti .... doctor?
   No, she isn't. She's a nurse.
4 .... Nevada?
   It's in the USA.
5 .... your phone from China?
   Yes, it is.
6 .... your name ?
   It's Nick.
7 .... Jan .... ?
   He's from Poland.
8 .... 'obrigada' in English?
   It's 'thank you'.
9 .... your hotel in Valetta?
   No, it isn't. It's in Sliema.

GRAMMAR BANK

1C How to … ask and answer simple questions

REFERENCE ◀◀ page 13

We use these questions to ask for basic information.

What's your	name? first name? surname? address? phone number?

We use these questions to ask about spelling.

How do you spell your	first name? surname?

We use these phrases for:

saying something is correct
That's right.
Perfect.
Great.

saying something is not correct
No, that's not right.
No, that's wrong.

saying 'please wait'
Just a moment.
Just a minute.

saying 'thank you'
Thank you.
Thanks.

We use these phrases to check an answer.

Sorry,	can you repeat that, please? is it D-O-Y-L-E? five or nine?

We use these titles for people.

person	we write	we say
a man	Mr	Mister
a woman	Ms	Mz /məz/
a married woman	Mrs	Missis
a single woman	Miss	Miss
a doctor	Dr	Doctor

PRACTICE

1 Put the words in the correct order to make a conversation.

A: ¹a / Hello, / student. / I'm / new
　　Hello, I'm a new student.
B: Hello. ²name? / your / What's
A: It's Denise Stratford.
B ³surname? / your / spell / you / do / How
A: S-T-R-A-T-F-O-R-D
B: Sorry, S-T-R-A-D … ?
A: ⁴that's / right. / No, / not / It's S-T-R-A-T …
B: OK. ⁵your / address? / What's
A: 5 Park Road, London N12.
B: Sorry. ⁶repeat / Can / please? / you / that,
A: 5 Park Road, London N12.
B: Thanks. ⁷minute. / a / Just / Here's your card.
A: Thank you.
B: ⁸Goodbye. / problem. / No

2 Correct the mistakes in the conversation.

A: What ~~are~~ 's your surname?
B: It's García.
A: What's you're first name?
B: Tomás.
A: Tomás García. Just a moment … Here it is. What's your phone numbers?
B: It's 322 6237.
A: Sorry, is he 322 6237?
B: That's right.
A: What your address?
B: 7 Monroe Street, Washington.
A: How do you sing the street name?
B: M-O-N-R-O-E.
A: OK, great, thanks you. Here's your key card. You're in room 931.
B: Thank you.

3 Use the prompts to make a conversation.

A: morning. / What / name?
　　Good morning. What's your name?
B: Hello. / name / be / Kumar. / Nadia Kumar.
A: How / spell / Nadia?
B: N-A-D-I-A.
A: you / repeat / surname, / please?
B: Kumar.
A: Be / K-U-M-E-R?
B: No / that / not right. / It / be / K-U-M-A-R.
A: Just / minute. / Here's your card, Ms Kumar.
B: Perfect. / Thank

94

GRAMMAR BANK

1D singular and plural nouns; *a*, *an*; *have*, *has*

REFERENCE ◀◀ page 14

Singular nouns

We use *a* and *an* with:
- singular nouns.
  a pen, an email
- adjectives and singular nouns.
  a big supermarket
  an Italian café

We use *a* + a word beginning with a consonant sound.
a phone, **a T**urkish restaurant, **a h**otel

We use *an* + a word beginning with a vowel sound.
an actor, **an o**ffice worker, **an A**ustralian bank

Plural nouns

We use *-s*, *-es* and *-ies* to make nouns **plural**.
ticket**s**, box**es**, countr**ies**

Spelling of regular plurals

most nouns	
add **-s**	passport**s**
	key**s**
nouns ending *-ch*, *-s*, *-ss*, *-sh*, *-x*	
add **-es**	watch**es**
	bus**es**
	glass**es**
	dish**es**
	box**es**
nouns ending consonant + *-y*, e.g. *university*, *country*	
change to **-ies**	universit**ies**
	countr**ies**

Notice that we say:
a university, **a** UK passport
NOT ~~an university, an UK passport~~
office workers, big problems
NOT ~~office*s* workers; big*s* problems~~

We use *the* when we have only one thing in a place.
the teacher, look at **the** board, close **the** door

have / has

We use *have* for possession.

I You	have	a passport.
He She It	has	an English name.

PRACTICE

1 Write *a* or *an* before the nouns.

1. .... photo
2. .... restaurant
3. .... Indian name
4. .... nationality
5. .... phone number
6. .... address
7. .... shop assistant
8. .... American city
9. .... taxi driver
10. .... sandwich

2 Write the plural form of the words in Ex 1.

1. photos
2. ....
3. ....
4. ....
5. ....
6. ....
7. ....
8. ....
9. ....
10. ....

3 Look at the pictures and complete the sentences. Use *a* or *an* or the correct number.

I have …

1. two bags.
2. ....

3. ....
4. ....

My city has …

5. ....
6. ....

7. ....
8. ....

GRAMMAR BANK

2A present simple *be*: *we, you, they*

REFERENCE ⏪ page 19

We use *you* for one person or for two, three, four, etc., people.

Positive (+)

subject	be	phrase
We	're	Spanish.
You	are	actors.
They		married.

We use **'** for a missing letter.

We ~~a~~re → We're   You ~~a~~re → You're   They ~~a~~re → They're

We use contractions (*we're, you're, they're*) in speaking and in emails and messages to friends.
We're waiters. **You're** happy. **They're** from Italy.

Negative (-)

subject	be + not	phrase
We	aren't	from the UK.
You	are not	students.
They		old.

We use a contraction (*they aren't*) in speaking and in emails and messages to friends. They **aren't** Polish.

We can also say *We're not, You're not, They're not.*
We're not tired. **You're not** young. **They're not** new.

Yes/No questions

They are actors.   Are they actors?

be	subject	phrase
Are	we	in Paris?
	you	from Colombia?
	they	office workers?

Short answers

Yes/No	subject	be
Yes,	we	are.
	you	
No,	they	aren't.

We don't use contractions with short answers with *yes*.
Yes, we are. NOT ~~Yes, we're.~~

We can also say *No, we're not.*

Wh- questions

Wh- question word	be	subject
Who	are	we?
Where		they from?

PRACTICE

1 Choose the correct alternative.

A: This is a photo of Ruby and Max.
B: Are ¹**you** / **we** friends?
A: Yes, ²**we** / **we're** friends from university.
B: ³**Are you** / **they** married?
A: Yes, ⁴**they are** / **they're**.
B: ⁵**Are they** / **Are** British?
A: No, ⁶**aren't** / **they aren't**.
B: Where ⁷**they are** / **are they** from?
A: ⁸**They** / **They're** from Australia.

2 Change the phrases in bold to *we*, *they* or *you*. Write the complete sentence.

1 **Harry and Tony** are singers.
   They're singers.
2 **Julie and I** are shop assistants.
   ....
3 Are **Camille and Sara** from Scotland?
   ....
4 **My teachers** are Mr Vega and Ms Fox.
   ....
5 Where are **you and Paola**?
   ....
6 **The nurses** aren't here.
   ....
7 **Len and I** are at university.
   ....
8 Are **your phone numbers** here?
   ....

3 Complete the conversation with the words in the box.

| are (x2)   's   I   it's   'm   n't   're |
| what   where   we   we're   you |

A: Hi. My name ¹ _'s_ Alex.
B: ² ....'s your name?
C: ³ ....'m Bridget. I ⁴ .... married to Alex.
B: ⁵ .... are you from?
A: ⁶ .... from Switzerland.
B: Where are ⁷ .... today?
C: Today we ⁸ .... in Argentina.
B: ⁹ .... you in Buenos Aires?
A: No, we are ¹⁰ .... ¹¹ .... 're in Puerto Iguazú.
C: Yes, ¹² .... beautiful here.
A: And the people ¹³ .... really friendly.
B: Have a good day!
A/C: Thanks.

GRAMMAR BANK

2B possessive adjectives

REFERENCE ◀◀ page 21

"My name's Pete"

His name's Andy.

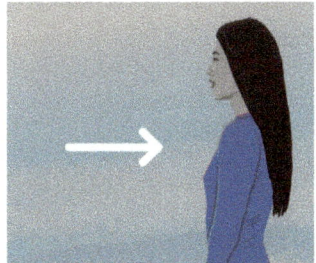
Her name's Diana.

Its name's Boots.

Our surname's Lucas.

Their names are Suzie and Phil.

subject pronoun	possessive adjective
I	my
you	your
he	his
she	her
it	its
we	our
they	their

We use possessive adjectives before nouns.
Where's **my book**?
What are **their names**?
Our lesson is in room 23.

We say *your books*, *their names*, *our lessons*.
NOT ~~yours books~~, ~~theirs names~~, ~~ours lessons~~
We use *its* for things and animals.

Notice the spelling.
It's = *It is*. It's a cat.
Its = possessive. Its name is Boots.

They're = *They are*. They're my parents.
Their = possessive. Their names are Zhang Wei and Li Na.

You're = *You are*. You're in room 52.
Your = possessive. What's your surname?

PRACTICE

1 Choose the correct alternative.

A: Hi, is today ¹**your / you** first day at school?
B: Yes. Are you ²**your / my** teacher?
A: No, I'm a student. ³**Our / We** teacher isn't here.
B: What's ⁴**our / her** name?
A: ⁵**Our / Her** teacher is a man. ⁶**His / Her** name is Mr Santo.
B: Where is ⁷**he / she**?
A: ⁸**He's / His** in the office, with the other teachers.
B: Where is ⁹**they're / their** office?
A: ¹⁰**It's / Its** in room 515.

2 Correct the conversations. Add two words from the box.

| ~~my~~ his her its our your (x2) their |

1 A: Hello, *my* name's Thalia.
   B: Hi, Thalia.
   A: What are names?
   B: I'm Adam and this is Janine.

2 A: This is a photo of children.
   B: What are names?
   A: Maya and Penny.
   B: Oh, they're beautiful!

3 A: Is Lorraine married?
   B: Yes, husband's a businessman with a big company.
   A: What's name?
   B: Samsung.
   A: Samsung's a very big company!

4 A: Hi Liz, I'm at the airport, but brother isn't here.
   B: Oh, no. Just a moment. I have phone number.
   A: Thanks.
   B: It's 035927 4832725.

GRAMMAR BANK

2C How to ... have short conversations

REFERENCE ⏪ page 23

We use *How* questions to start conversations.

How's How is	work? school? your new phone? your sister?
How are	you? your children? your classes? things?

We use these phrases to answer.

It's I'm He's She's We're They're	good/great! OK/not bad.
	Not very good. Fine.

We use these phrases to start conversations.

starting a conversation	responding
Hi, Kate! Are you OK? It's a beautiful day.	Hi. Yes, I'm well. Yes, it is.

We use these phrases to end conversations.

ending a conversation	responding
Look at the time! Thanks for the coffee. See you later.	No problem. See you./Bye.

Other useful phrases:

A:	B:
Coffee?	No, thanks. Yes, please. Black, please. White, no sugar.
I'm tired.	Me too.

PRACTICE

1 Match the question (1–8) with the answers (a–h).

1 How's your job? **f**
2 How's university?
3 How's your apartment?
4 How's your brother?
5 How's your mother?
6 How are things?
7 How are your parents?
8 How's your new cat?

a He's OK.
b It's great. It's small but it's in the city.
c It's beautiful. Its name is Mitzy.
d Not bad but I'm very tired. My brother's not OK and my apartment is very small.
e They're fine, thank you. My mother's fifty now.
f It's great, thanks. The people in the office are very friendly.
g I'm very happy with it. My classes are difficult, but they're good.
h She's great, thank you.

2 Choose TWO correct answers for each conversation.

1 A: Are you OK?
 B: **Yes, I'm well.** / No, thanks. / **I'm fine, thanks.**

2 A: See you later.
 B: **No problem.** / **Bye.** / **See you.**

3 A: How's your sister?
 B: **She's OK.** / It's not very good. / **She's fine.**

4 A: Coffee?
 B: **White, no sugar.** / **Black, please.** / It's great!

5 A: It's a beautiful day.
 B: Yes, I'm well. / **Yes, it is.** / **Yes.**

6 A: How's your new phone?
 B **I'm very happy with it.** / **It's not bad.** / They're good.

3 Put the words in the correct order to make a conversation.

Maria: ¹nice / Kemi, / see / Hi, / to / you.
  Hi, Kemi, nice to see you.
Kemi: ²things? / are / Maria. / Hi, / How
Maria: ³thanks. / Good, / Coffee?
Kemi: ⁴please. / Yes, / sugar. / Black, / no
Maria: ⁵are / children? / your / How
Kemi: ⁶well. / 're / very / They
Maria: ⁷the / Thanks / for / coffee.
Kemi: ⁸problem. / No

4 Complete the conversation.

Oskar: Hi Yusuf, good ¹ __to__ see you.
Yusuf: Hi Oskar, how ² _____ you?
Oskar: I ³ _____ fine, thanks. You?
Yusuf: Me ⁴ _____ . How ⁵ _____ your mother?
Oskar: ⁶ _____ 's OK, thank you. How's ⁷ _____ new apartment?
Yusuf: ⁸ _____ 's great. We're ⁹ _____ happy with it.
Oskar: Good. Look at the ¹⁰ _____ ! Thanks ¹¹ _____ the chat.
Yusuf: ¹² _____ you later.
Oskar: Bye.

GRAMMAR BANK

2D wh- questions + be

REFERENCE ◀◀ page 25

What?

Who?

Where?

When?

How?

How old?

We use wh- question words and be to ask questions about:
- a thing.   A: **What's** in your bag?   B: My laptop.
- a person. A: **Who** are your teachers?   B: Stuart and Emma.
- a place.   A: **Where** is Tennessee?   B: In the USA.
- a time.   A: **When's** our class?   B: At ten o'clock.
- manner.   A: **How** are your parents?   B: They're well.
- age.   A: **How old** is Stefan?   B: He's fifteen.

wh- question word	be	subject or phrase
What	's	Gideon's job?
	are	their names?
Who	's	your friend?
	are	you?
Where	am	I?
	's	Leyla from?
	are	my pens?
When	's	her birthday?
	are	their classes?
How	's	Gianna?
	are	you today?
How old	's	his car?
	are	his children?

We use contractions (*What's, Who's, Where's, When's, How's*) in speaking, in emails and in messages to friends.
What's her name? **Where's** she from?

We also often use the full form.
What is her name? **Where is** she from?

PRACTICE

1 Complete the questions with the words in the box.

> How's   How are   ~~What's~~   What are   When
> When's   Who's   Who are   Where's   Where are

1 <u>What's</u> your email address?
   It's domway34@hetmail.ac.com.
2 .... Verona?
   It's in Italy.
3 .... your parents?
   They're Michael and Sheila.
4 .... your new car?
   It's great! I'm very happy with it.
5 .... the answers to Exercise 3A?
   Number 1 is 'a', number 2 is 'an' and number 3 is 'a'.
6 .... our English class?
   It's on Wednesday.
7 .... Kiera?
   She's my wife.
8 .... your children?
   They're at school.
9 .... your classes?
   They're difficult, but they're great!
10 .... is the weekend in your country?
   It's on Friday and Saturday.

2 Correct the mistake in each question.

1 A: ~~What~~ are Diana and Kayla?
   Who are Diana and Kayla?
   B: They're my sisters.
   A: When are they?
   B: They're very young, two and five.

2 A: How's 'fútbol' in English?
   B: It's 'football'.
   A: What's your favourite football player?
   B: Cristiano Ronaldo.

3 A: How old has Tom?
   B: He's twenty-two.
   A: Who's he now?
   B: He's at university in Toronto, Canada.

4 A: When are the children?
   B: They're in the park.
   A: What are they with?
   B: They're with Rosa.

GRAMMAR BANK

3A possessive 's

REFERENCE ◀◀ page 29

Suzanne's car

Joe's guitar

We use 's with a person.
Mrs Taylor's book
my brother's job

We use 's to talk about possessions.
Harry's watch is very old.
NOT ~~The watch of Harry is very old.~~

We use 's to talk about family.
He is **Maria's** son.
Jason's sister is an artist.

Notice that we also use 's with contractions.
Suzanne's from France = **Suzanne is** from France.
Joe's a businessman = **Joe is** a businessman.

possessive 's
↑
Pat's new **phone's** very good.
↓
contraction 's = is

PRACTICE

1 Correct the sentences. Add the possessive 's.
  1 This is Tom key.
     This is Tom's key.
  2 Anna favourite thing is her phone.
  3 Saanvi is Kiara mother.
  4 Our teacher name is Mr Kaminski.
  5 Katie taxi is here.
  6 Where are Luis glasses?
  7 Will Brown book is very good.
  8 Is this Jess magazine?
  9 Are you Ms McKee students?
  10 What is Michele address?

2 Correct the conversations. Add apostrophes (').
  1 A: ¹Whats your friends name?
       What's your friend's name?
     B: ²Its Alfonso.
     A: ³Is Alfonsos wifes name Gianna?
     B: ⁴No, her names Bella. Giannas their new baby.

  2 A: ⁵Your bags very big. Whats in it?
     B: ⁶I have my husbands laptop and my sons schoolbooks. His name is Rob. And I have a football!
     A: ⁷Is it Robs football?
     B: ⁸No, its my daughters football!

  3 A: ⁹Wheres Kirsties boyfriend from?
     B: ¹⁰Mikes from Dublin.
     A: ¹¹How olds Mike?
     B: ¹²I don't know. Twenty-eight? Jan, whens Mikes birthday?

3 Look at Ex 2 again. Is each 's possessive 's (P) or a contraction of *is* (C)?
  1 What's C, friend's P
  2
  3
  4
  5
  6
  7
  8
  9
  10
  11
  12

GRAMMAR BANK

3B present simple *have* + yes/no questions (*I, you, we, they*)

REFERENCE ⏪ page 31

We use *have* in the present simple to talk about possessions (things), friends and family.
I **have** a new bike. We **have** two friends in Rome.
Sam and Mina **have** three children.

Positive

subject	have	object or phrase
I	have	a new phone.
You		an Italian father.
We		three sisters.
They		some photos.

With the positive *have* we use:
- *a/an* + singular nouns.
  They **have a daughter**.
  You **have an email** from Nicola.
- numbers + singular or plural nouns.
  I **have one brother** and **three sisters**.
- *some* + plural nouns.
  I **have some keys**.

three keys

some keys

Negative

subject	auxiliary (*do*)	have	object
I	don't	have	a big TV.
You	do not		an English book.
We			two classes today.
They			any brothers.

We use the contraction *don't* (= *do not*) in speaking and in emails and messages to friends. I **don't have** a car.

With the negative *don't have* we use:
- *a, an*, numbers.
  I **don't have a job**. We **don't have an office**. They **don't have two cars**.
- *any* + plural nouns.
  Mel and Tim **don't have any** brothers. (= no brothers)

Yes/No questions

auxiliary verb (*do*)	subject	have	object
Do	you	have	a car?
	they		any British friends?

With yes/no questions we use:
- *a, an* + singular nouns. Do you have **a pen**?
  Do you have **an American** passport?
- *any* + plural nouns. Do you have **any tissues**?

Short answers

Yes/No	subject	auxiliary verb (*do*)
Yes,	I	do.
No,	we	don't.

No, they don't. NOT ~~No, they don't have.~~

PRACTICE

1 Complete the sentences with *a, an, some* or *any*.
1. I have __a__ Spanish passport and _____ English passport.
2. Do you have _____ menu?
3. We have _____ Chinese students in the class.
4. Do they have _____ friends in the UK?
5. I have _____ old phone.
6. You don't have _____ bags with you.
7. We have _____ scissors, but where are they?
8. Do they have _____ sandwiches in the café?

2 Put the words in the correct order to make questions.
1. a / you / bike? / Do / have Do you have a bike?
2. children? / Pat and Viv / Do / have / any
3. at / you / Nasir, / desk / a / do / have / home?
4. cups? / we / any / do / have / Carolina,
5. have / Craig? / any / you / Do / sisters,
6. Davies, / have / any / Mrs / do / books? / the students

3 Complete the short answers to the questions (1–6) in Ex 2.
1. No, I don't.
2. Yes, _____ .
3. Yes, _____ .
4. No, _____ .
5. Yes, _____ .
6. No, _____ .

4 Correct one mistake in each line of the conversations.
1. A: Do you have ~~any~~ **a** laptop at home?
   B: No, I do, but I have a tablet.
   A: And do you a phone?
   B: Yes, I don't, but it's not here.
2. A: Do you have some children?
   B: Yes, we do have. We have two boys.
   A: Do they have any photos?
   B: Yes, here on my phone. They have six and eight.

GRAMMAR BANK

3C How to ... shop for clothes

REFERENCE ◀◀ page 33

We use *How much* to ask about prices.

How much	is the coat?
	is this jumper?
	are the shoes?

We use these answers.

It's	five euros (€5).
	eighteen dollars ($18).
They're	twenty-five pounds (£25).

We use these phrases when buying clothes.

customer	shop assistant
Excuse me?	Can I help you?
Can I try this jacket on?	Yes, of course.
Can I try it on?	
Do you have a small size?	Yes, we do.
	No, we don't.
	Yes. Here you are.
Where's the changing room?	It's over there.

We use these phrases to talk about size.
Extra small/XS
Small/S
Medium/M
Large/L
Extra large/XL
Size ten/10
I'm (a) size sixteen.

PRACTICE

1 Choose the correct alternative.

A: Excuse ¹**I / me**?
B: Yes, ²**I can / Can I** help you?
A: Yes, how much ³**is / are** this coat?
B: ⁴**It's / Its** €37.
A: Do you have a medium ⁵**colour / size**?
B: Yes, here ⁶**you're / you are**.
A: Can I ⁷**have / try** it on?
B: Yes, ⁸**course / of course**.
A: And how much ⁹**is / are** the shoes?
B: ¹⁰**They / They're** €43. What size are ¹¹**you / they**?
A: ¹²**I'm / My** size 40.

2 Complete the conversation.

A: This top is nice. How ¹ _much_ is it?
B: I don't know. ² _____ me?
C: Yes? Can I ³ _____ you?
B: ⁴ _____ much is this top?
C: It ⁵ _____ £12.99.
A: That's good. Can I try it ⁶ _____ ?
C: Yes, of ⁷ _____ .
A: Do you ⁸ _____ a small size?
C: Yes, ⁹ _____ you are.
A: Thanks. Where's the ¹⁰ _____ room?
C: It's over there.

3 Use the prompts to make a conversation.

GRAMMAR BANK

3D likes, dislikes and opinions

REFERENCE ◀◀ page 34

I **love** old cars.

I **like** old cars.

I **don't like** old cars.

I **hate** old cars.

We use *love, like, don't like, hate* with:

- plural nouns.
  I love **shoes**. They hate big **shops**.

- the names of people and places.
  I like **Fatima**. We love **Spain**.

- nouns that don't have a plural.*
  I love **football**. My children don't like **homework**.

* Some other nouns that don't have a plural are: *music, money, rain, water, work, tennis, golf, information, the internet.*

We use *really* before *like, love, don't like, hate*.
I **really** like food shops. I **really** don't like clothes shops.

We use *a lot* after *like* + object. I like Pat **a lot**.

We use *think* for opinions.

I love it. I **think** it's beautiful.

I don't like it. I **think** it's really bad.

Yes/No questions

auxiliary (*do*)	subject	infinitive	object or phrase
Do	I you we they	like	children?
		think	this app is good?

Short answers

Yes/No	subject	auxiliary (*do*)
Yes,	I	do.
No,	they	don't.

No, I **don't**. NOT ~~No, I don't like.~~

PRACTICE

1 Choose the correct alternative.

1 I **love** / **hate** coffee. It's my favourite thing in the morning.
2 Do you **love** / **like** Pete's girlfriend? I think she's nice.
3 Our parents like everything new. They **really** / **don't** like old things.
4 I **hate** / **not like** my job! It's really difficult.
5 I **like** / **think** this photo of you is beautiful.
6 Stuart and I **very** / **really** like Turkey.
7 I have an orange phone, an orange car and an orange laptop. I **love** / **like a lot** orange!
8 My children like their new teacher a **much** / **lot**.
9 Do you **think** / **like** this book is good?
10 Mimi and Alessio **no** / **don't** like cities.

2 Put the words in the correct order to make conversations.

1 A: week? / your / day / favourite / the / of / What's
   What's your favourite day of the week?
   B: I / Fridays. / like / really
   A: too. / Me
   B: hate / Mondays. / And / I / really

2 A: coat? / like / my / Sonia, / new / you / do
   B: do. / Yes, / I / it's / beautiful. / think / I
   A: new / your / How's / apartment?
   B: happy / We're / with / it. / really / We / lot. / like / a / it

3 Correct the mistake in each sentence. Two sentences are correct.

1 I love clothes shop.
   I love clothes shops.
2 We like really bookshops.
3 Young people no like black and white films.
4 We hate big city.
5 Mark and Sheila like Mexico a lot.
6 Think you the new supermarket is good?
7 I not think Julia's ring is old.
8 A: Do you like babies? B: Yes, I like.
9 We don't like football, but we love tennis.
10 I like your coat lot.
11 Like Tom and Kate Italian restaurants?
12 We like a lot our new apartment.

GRAMMAR BANK

4A adverbs of frequency

REFERENCE ◀◀ page 39

We use the present simple to talk about:
- possessions, likes, dislikes and opinions.
  We **have** six apples.
  My children **really like** pizzas.
  I **think** Sofia is a great restaurant.
- habits and routines.
  I **have** breakfast at seven.
  Do you **eat** fish every day?

We use adverbs of frequency to talk about habits and routines.

never	not often	sometimes	often	usually	always
0%	20%	40%	60%	80%	100%

Positive

subject	adverb of frequency	verb	object or phrase
I You We They	always never	drink	coffee at breakfast.
		eat	fish at lunch.

Adverbs of frequency go before a verb.
I **always have** an egg for breakfast.
NOT ~~I have always an egg for breakfast.~~
have = eat or drink
I **often have** a sandwich and a fruit juice for lunch.

Negative

subject	auxiliary (do)	adverb of frequency	verb	object or phrase
I You We They	don't	usually often	drink	tea with milk.
			have	fish for breakfast.

We use a positive (+) verb with *never*.
We **never eat** in restaurants.
NOT ~~We don't never eat in restaurants.~~

Yes/No questions and adverbs of frequency

auxiliary (do)	subject	adverb of frequency	verb	object or phrase
Do	you they	usually often	eat	red meat?

We use normal short answers.
Yes, I do.
No, we don't.

PRACTICE

1 Put the adverbs of frequency in brackets in the correct place.

1 I drink tea with milk. (never)
   I never drink tea with milk.
2 We have breakfast at eight. (usually)
3 My parents eat dinner at nine. (always)
4 I have an umbrella in my bag. (not often)
5 My children listen to the radio. (never)
6 I choose green apples. (often)
7 Do you write in a notebook? (always)
8 I look at our old family photos. (sometimes)
9 I read newspapers. (not usually)
10 Do Barry and Olivia speak Spanish? (often)

2 Look at the table. Complete the conversation with the correct adverbs of frequency.

	Mon	Tues	Wed	Thurs	Fri	Sat	Sun
meat or fish		✓				✓	✓
vegetables	✓		✓		✓		✓
fruit	✓	✓	✓	✓	✓	✓	✓
tea	✓	✓		✓	✓	✓	✓
coffee							
chocolate						✓	

A: Do you eat healthy food?
B: Yes, good food is very important to me. I ¹ _always_ have fruit for breakfast.
A: Do you drink tea or coffee?
B: I ² _____ drink tea, but I ³ _____ drink coffee.
A: Do you like vegetables?
B: I like vegetables and I ⁴ _____ eat green vegetables or tomatoes and pasta for lunch.
A: Do you eat meat?
B: I ⁵ _____ eat meat or fish and I ⁶ _____ eat meat or fish at the weekend.
A: And do you always eat healthy food?
B: Well, I love chocolate, but I don't ⁷ _____ eat it. I ⁸ _____ have it at the weekend, but not always.

GRAMMAR BANK

4B present simple: regular verbs (he, she, it)

REFERENCE ◀◀ page 41

Positive

subject	infinitive (+ -s, -es)	object or phrase
He She It	starts finishes	at nine. at six.

Spelling

most verbs	add -s	read**s** make**s**
verbs ending -ch, -sh, -ss, -x	add -es	finish**es** watch**es**
do and go	add -es	do**es** go**es**
verbs ending consonant + -y e.g. study, try	change to -ies	stud**ies** tr**ies**
have	irregular	**has**

Negative

subject	auxiliary verb (do)	infinitive	object or phrase
He She It	doesn't	eat	meat.
		have	breakfast.

She lik**es** football.   She do**es**n't like football.

We use the contraction *doesn't* (= *does not*) for negatives in speaking and in informal writing.

Diana **doesn't work** on Mondays.

Notice that we use adverbs of frequency before a verb.

Nick **sometimes gets up** at half past five.
Dylan **never has** breakfast.
Jayne **doesn't often watch** TV.

PRACTICE

1 Write the correct present simple form of the verbs in bold.

MP's weekends are different. She usually ¹**get up** <u>gets up</u> at 10, and she ²**have** a big breakfast. She always ³**check** her emails. She ⁴**answer** important emails and then she ⁵**do** something outside. For example, she ⁶**work** in the garden. On Saturday, MP often ⁷**make** dinner for her family. 'After dinner, MP's brother ⁸**choose** a film and he ⁹**watch** it with MP. She ¹⁰**go** to bed early – at 10 or 10.30. She sometimes ¹¹**read** in bed, but she never ¹²**look at** her emails and messages at night.

2 Complete the sentences with the correct form of the verbs in brackets.
1 My brother Tom <u>doesn't drink</u> (not drink) coffee, but he .... (love) fruit juice.
2 My father .... (make) breakfast for everyone at seven and he .... (go) to work at eight.
3 My sister Lorna .... (not like) the colour red, but she .... (have) one red T-shirt.
4 My friend Tess .... (understand) English, but she .... (not speak) it.
5 My mother .... (not eat) breakfast. She .... (read) her emails and messages and has a cup of black coffee.
6 My friend Leo never .... (work) in the evening, but he sometimes .... (study) Spanish.
7 Mrs White .... (not know) my name, but she always .... (say) hello.
8 My doctor .... (ask) a lot of questions and he always .... (listen) to my answers.

3 Correct the mistake in each sentence. Two sentences are correct.
1 Marko live in Vienna.
   <u>Marko lives in Vienna.</u>
2 Dr Lund doesn't likes it.
3 Rachel studys in the evening.
4 My sister doesn't often have lunch.
5 My brother no hates cats.
6 Ms Rodriguez starts work always at eight o'clock.
7 Sam never doesn't write emails.
8 Tessa doesn't usually leave home at nine.
9 Mr Hart think phones are bad in class.
10 My son gos to bed at nine o'clock.

105

GRAMMAR BANK

4C How to … order in a café

REFERENCE ◀◀ page 43

We use this language to order food and drink in a café.

| Can I have
Can we have | a tea,
a pastry,
two coffees, | please? |

We use *How much* to ask about price.

| How much is | this pastry?
it?
that? |

We often use *that* to ask about the price of all the food and drink.

Can we have three coffees and an apple pastry, please?
How much is **that**?

We use these phrases to answer about price.

It's two euros.
That's ten dollars.

The waiter says:
Can I help you?
Anything else?
Here you are.
Here you go.
Just a moment.
Just a minute.
Let me check.

We ask about alternatives with *or*.

question			answer
Still	or	sparkling?	Still, please.
Tea		coffee?	Tea, please.

PRACTICE

1 Put the words in the correct order to make sentences.
1 have / I / a / Can / coffee, / please?
   Can I have a coffee, please?
2 is / much / it? / How
3 one / fifty. / It's / pound
4 moment. / Just / a
5 you / go. / Here
6 Can / pastries, / four / we / please? / have
7 check. / me / Let
8 you / Here / are.

2 Complete the conversation with the words in the box. There are two extra words.

| a   can   cold   else   help   much |
| or   please   no   that   that's   we |

A: Can I ¹_____ you?
B: Yes, ²_____ we have two egg sandwiches, ³_____ ?
A: White ⁴_____ brown bread?
B: Brown, please.
A: Anything ⁵_____ ?
B: Yes, can ⁶_____ have two Americanos, with milk?
A: Hot or ⁷_____ milk?
B: Hot, please. How much is ⁸_____ ?
A: Just ⁹_____ minute … ¹⁰_____ nine pounds fifty.

3 Complete the conversations.
1 A: Can I ¹help you?
   B: Yes, can I have a ²k_____ and ³f_____ , please?
   A: ⁴J_____ a moment. Here you go.
   B: Thank you.
   A: I'm sorry about that.
   B: No problem. Can we have two ⁵m_____ waters, please?
   A: Still or ⁶s_____ ?
   B: Still, please.

2 A: Excuse ⁷m_____ ? Can I have a napkin, please?
   B: Of course. ⁸H_____ you are.
   A: Thank you. How ⁹m_____ are the pastries?
   B: They're three ¹⁰e_____ .
   A: Can I have two, please?
   B: Apple ¹¹o_____ chocolate?
   A: An apple ¹²p_____ , please.

106

GRAMMAR BANK

4D present simple: yes/no questions (he, she, it)

REFERENCE ◀ page 45

Yes/No questions

She eat**s** meat. → Do**es** she eat meat?

auxiliary verb (*does*)	subject	infinitive	object or phrase
Does	he	live	in Brazil?
	she	like	animals?
	it	start	at nine?

Does he live here?
NOT ~~Does he lives here?~~

Short answers to *yes/no* questions.

Yes/No	subject	auxiliary verb (*do*)
Yes,	he	does.
No,	it	doesn't.

No, it doesn't.
NOT ~~No, it doesn't start.~~

PRACTICE

1 Put the words in the correct order to make questions.
  1 job? / son / like / your / his / Does
    Does your son like his job?
  2 pastries? / Megan / like / Does
  3 Mrs Wood / Italian? / Does / speak
  4 Julia / Does / write /often / you? / to
  5 children? / any / Mr Baker / Does / have
  6 have / your / good / Matt, / a / phone / does / camera?
  7 Liz, / you? / mother / does / live / your / with
  8 at / lesson / start / does / the / Tessa, / nine?

2 Match the questions (1–8) in Ex 1 with the answers (a–h).
  a ✓ _Yes, he does_ . He has a son and a daughter. 5
  b ✓ _____ . She writes every week.
  c ✗ _____ . It starts at ten.
  d ✓ _____ . He thinks his job's great.
  e ✗ _____ . But she speaks Spanish.
  f ✓ _____ . It's really good.
  g ✗ _____ . She has an apartment in town.
  h ✓ _____ . She really loves pastries.

3 Write the short answers in Ex 2.

4 Complete the questions with *Does*, *Do*, *Is* or *Are*.
  1 _Does_ Himari drink milk?
  2 _____ your children like fish?
  3 _____ Jerry's wallet black?
  4 _____ the class finish at eight o'clock?
  5 _____ Henning and Mia understand English?
  6 _____ your shoes from Germany?
  7 _____ Kasia's surname start with a 'W' or a 'V'?
  8 _____ it half past nine now?

5 Use the prompts to make conversations.
  1 A: Be / your brother / teacher?
      Is your brother a teacher?
     B: No / he / be / not. / He / be / businessman.
     A: he / like / his job?
     B: No, / he / not.
     A: he / work / in the city?
     B: Yes, / he
     A: Be / he / married?
     B: No / he / not.

  2 A: Be / your Chinese classes good?
     B: Yes, / they / be.
     A: your teacher / speak / English?
     B: Yes, / she / but she / never / speak / English in class.
     A: Be / Chinese easy?
     B: No / it / be / not, / but I love it!
     A: you / understand / everything in class?
     B: Yes, / I / but I / not understand / films in Chinese.

107

VOCABULARY BANK

LEAD-IN

international words

⏪ page 6

1 A Match the words (1–10) with the photos (A–J).

1 ..... a bank
2 ..... a camera
3 ..... a computer
4 ..... a menu
5 ..... a hotel
6 ..... a passport
7 ..... a phone
8 ..... a supermarket
9 ..... a taxi
10 ..... a university

B 🔊 VB.L.01 | Look at the photos again. Listen and repeat.

C Work in pairs. Student A: Point to a photo. Student B: Say the word.

classroom language

⏪ page 6

1 A Match the verbs and phrases (1–10) with the pictures (A–L).

1 ..... answer
2 ..... ask
3 ..... check your answers
4 ..... choose
5 ..... listen
6 ..... look at
7 ..... match
8 ..... read
9 ..... write
10 ..... say 'hello'
11 ..... work alone
12 ..... work in pairs

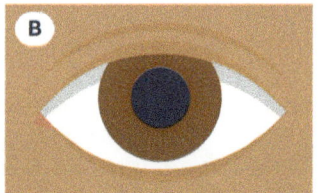
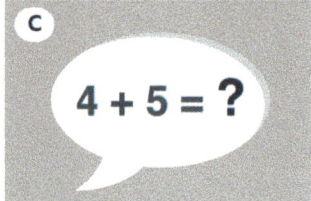
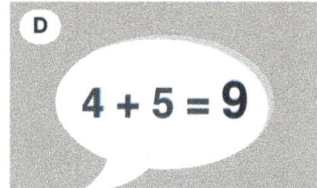

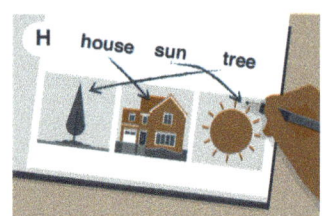

B 🔊 VB.L.02 | Look at the pictures again. Listen and repeat.

C Work in groups. Student A: Say a classroom instruction. Other students: Do the action.

VOCABULARY BANK

1A countries and nationalities

◀◀ page 9

1 A Complete the table (1–14) with the correct nationalities.

B 🔊 **VB1.01** | Listen and underline the stressed syllable in each country or nationality.

C 🔊 **VB1.01** | Listen again and repeat.

D Work in pairs. Student A: Say a country. Student B: Say the nationality.

A: Italy.
B: Italian.

country	nationality	country	nationality
	-an/-ian		-ish
Argentina	Argentinian	Poland	Polish
Australia	1	Spain	10 ....
Brazil	2	Turkey	11 ....
Colombia	3	the UK	12 ....
India	4		-ese
Italy	5	China	Chinese
Mexico	6	Vietnam	13 ....
the US/the USA	7	Japan	14 ....
South Africa	8		other
South Korea	9	France	French
		Germany	German
		Switzerland	Swiss

1B jobs

◀◀ page 10

1 A Match the jobs (1–10) with the photos (A–J).

1 ...... bus driver
2 ...... actor
3 ...... nurse
4 ...... police officer
5 ...... shop assistant
6 ...... office worker
7 ...... businessman, businesswoman
8 ...... digital designer
9 ...... football player
10 ...... artist

B 🔊 **VB1.02** | Look at the photos again. Listen and repeat.

2 A Look at the sentences. Choose the correct word to complete the rules.

I'm **a** bus driver. I'm **an** actor.

1 We use **a(n) / nothing** + jobs.
2 We use **a / an** + jobs beginning with a consonant sound (b, c, d, f …).
3 We use **a / an** + jobs beginning with a vowel sound (a, e, o …).

B Add *a* or *an* to the jobs in Ex 1A.

1 a bus driver 2 an actor

C 🔊 **VB1.03** | Listen and underline the stressed syllable(s) in each job.

a <u>bus</u> <u>dri</u>ver

3 A Work in pairs. Student A: Mime a job in Ex 1A. Student B: Guess the job.

B Complete the sentence with your job.

I'm a/an ....

VOCABULARY BANK

1D common objects

◀◀ page 14

1 A Match the words (1–13) with the photos (A–M).

1 ...... bag
2 ...... banana
3 ...... book
4 ...... bottle of water
5 ...... key
6 ...... laptop
7 ...... make-up
8 ...... mobile phone
9 ...... notebook
10 ...... purse
11 ...... sandwich
12 ...... umbrella
13 ...... wallet

B 🔊 VB1.04 | Listen and check.

C Work in pairs. Student A: Point to a photo. Student B: Say the word.

VOCABULARY BANK

2A common adjectives (1)
◂◂ page 19

1 A Match the adjectives (1–11) with the pictures (A–K).

1 ...... beautiful
2 ...... big and small
3 ...... easy and difficult
4 ...... favourite
5 ...... friendly
6 ...... good and bad
7 ...... happy and sad
8 ...... hot and cold
9 ...... new and old
10 ...... tired
11 ...... young and old

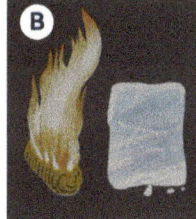

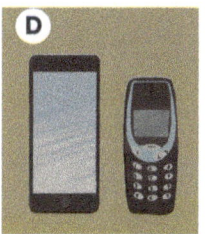

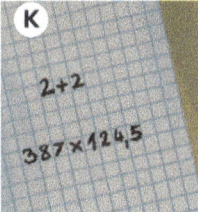

B 🔊 VB2.01 | Look at the pictures again. Listen and repeat.

C Work in pairs and test each other. Then swap roles.
1 Student A: Point to a picture in Ex 1A. Student B: Say the word or words.
2 Student A: Say one word in a word pair. Student B: Say the other word.

D Work in pairs. Student A: Choose an adjective from Ex 1A and say a noun that goes with it. Student B: Guess the adjective and say the phrase.

A: a coffee
B: a hot coffee

2B people
◂◂ page 21

1 A Match the people (1–8) with the photos (A–H).

1 ...... man
2 ...... woman
3 ...... child
4 ...... baby
5 ...... girl
6 ...... boy
7 ...... friend
8 ...... person

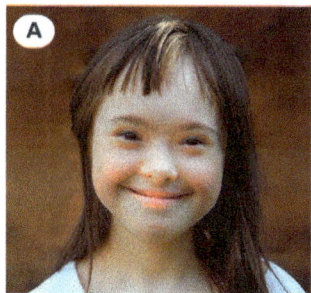

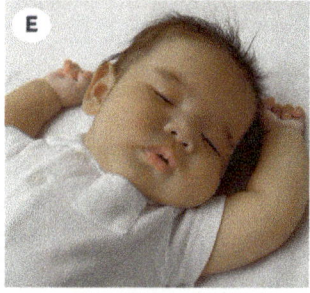

B 🔊 VB2.02 | Look at the photos again. Listen and repeat.

2 A Write the singular form.
1 people — *person*
2 men — ....
3 women — ....
4 children — ....

B 🔊 VB2.03 | Listen and repeat.

3 Work in pairs and test each other. Student A: Point to a photo in Ex 1A. Student B: Say the word.

VOCABULARY BANK

3A colours

◀◀ page 28

1 A Match the colours (1–10) with the pictures (A–J).

1 ...... black
2 ...... blue
3 ...... brown
4 ...... green
5 ...... orange
6 ...... pink
7 ...... purple
8 ...... red
9 ...... white
10 ...... yellow

B 🔊 **VB3.01** | Look at the pictures again. Listen and repeat.

C Match the colours (1–2) with the pictures (A–B).

1 **light** green
2 **dark** green

D 🔊 **VB3.02** | Listen and match the phrases (1–4) with the photos (A–D).

2 A Work in pairs. Student A: Point to a colour in Ex 1A. Student B: Say the colour.

B Work in pairs and take turns. Student A: Choose an object in the classroom. Say the colour. Student B: Guess the object.

A: yellow
B: Is it Maria's bag?

VOCABULARY BANK

VB

3C clothes

◀◀ page 32

1 A Match the clothes (1–12) with the photos (A–L).

1 ...... coat
2 ...... dress
3 ...... jacket
4 ...... jeans
5 ...... jumper
6 ...... shirt
7 ...... skirt
8 ...... suit
9 ...... top
10 ...... trousers
11 ...... T-shirt
12 ...... shoes

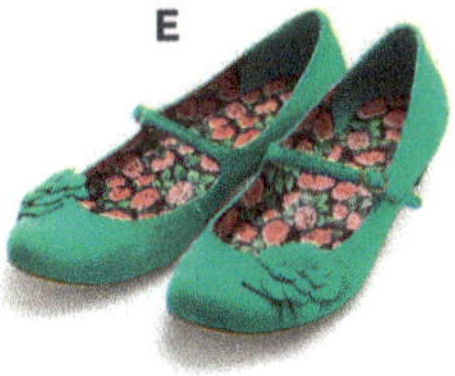

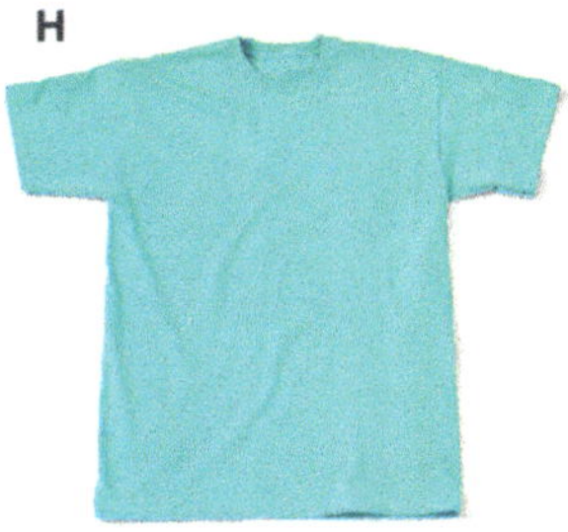

B 🔊 VB3.03 | Look at the photos again. Listen and repeat.

C Work in pairs. Close your books and look at the class. Write the clothes you see. Then compare your answers with other students.

D Match the sizes (1–3) with the photos (A–C).

1 small
2 medium
3 large

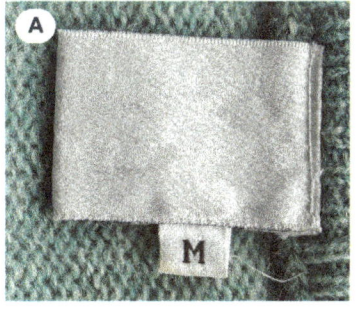
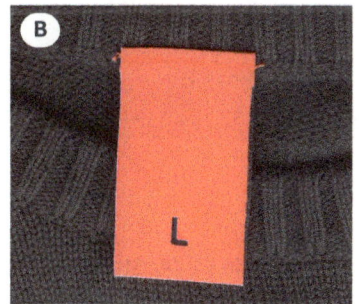

VOCABULARY BANK

3D shops
◀ page 34

1 A Match the words (1–10) with the photos (A–J).

1 ..... baker's 3 ..... butcher's 5 ..... computer shop 7 ..... shoe shop 9 ..... supermarket
2 ..... bookshop 4 ..... clothes shop 6 ..... pet shop 8 ..... sports shop 10 ..... video game shop

A

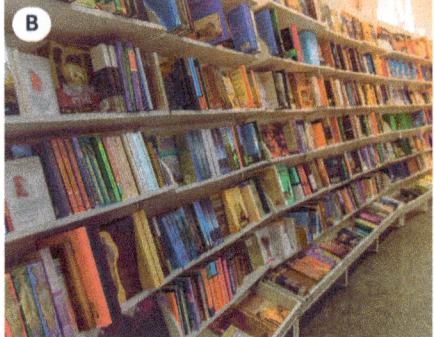
B

C

D

E

F

G

H

I

J

B 🔊 VB3.04 | Listen and check.

C Work in pairs. Student A: Point to a photo in Ex 1A. Student B: Say the word.

VOCABULARY BANK

VB

4A food and drink

◀◀ page 38

1 A Match the food and drink (1–20) with the photos (A–T).

Fruit
1. ...... apple
2. ...... banana
3. ...... orange

Vegetables
4. ...... carrot
5. ...... mushroom
6. ...... potato
7. ...... tomato

Meat
8. ...... steak
9. ...... beef
10. ...... chicken

Drinks
11. ...... milk
12. ...... fruit juice

Other
13. ...... pasta
14. ...... fish
15. ...... bread
16. ...... cereal
17. ...... rice
18. ...... cheese
19. ...... egg
20. ...... sandwich

B 🔊 VB4.01 | Listen and repeat.

C Write the plural form of the words for 1–8 and 19–20 in Ex 1A.

NOTICE Food and drink words (9–18) don't have plural forms,
e.g. *beef, pasta, fish, rice* NOT *beefs, pastas, rices*.

D Work in pairs. Choose the wrong item in each group.

1 apple	orange	(fish)	banana	Fish isn't a fruit.
2 carrot	mushroom	banana	potato	
3 milk	sandwich	fruit juice	water	
4 pasta	fruit juice	rice	potatoes	
5 steak	chicken	orange	beef	
6 banana	milk	potato	tomato	

2 A Cross out the alternative that is <u>wrong</u>.

1 I **have** / **eat** / **drink** fruit juice for breakfast.
2 I **have** / **eat** / **drink** eggs for breakfast.

B Work in pairs. What you eat and drink for breakfast?

A: I eat an egg and I drink tea. What do you have?

VOCABULARY BANK

4B telling the time

◀ page 40

1 A 🔊 VB4.02 | Listen to the times. Then listen and repeat.

  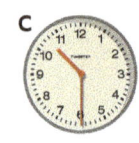

A ten o'clock   B quarter past ten   C half past ten

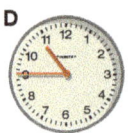 

D quarter to eleven   E eleven o'clock.

B Work in pairs. Ask and say the time for the pictures.

1  07.30
2
3  08.45
4  09.00
5
6  11.45
7
8  12.30

A: What's the time in number one?
B: It's half past seven. What's the time in … ?

2 A Choose the correct alternative.

1 **a.m. / p.m.** = in the morning from 12 midnight to 12 midday
2 **a.m. / p.m.** = in the afternoon and in the evening from 12 midday to 12 midnight

B Write six times. Use *a.m.* or *p.m.*

2 p.m., 4.30 a.m., 7.45 p.m.

C Work in pairs. Ask and answer about the times in Ex 2B. Write the times that your partner says.

A: What's the time?
B: It's 2 p.m.

D Work in pairs. Ask and answer the questions.

1 What time is it now?
2 What time is the English lesson?
3 When do people have dinner in your country?
4 When are the shops open in your town or city?

4C café words

◀ page 42

1 A Match the words (1–12) with the items in the photos (A–L).

1 ...... knife
2 ...... fork
3 ...... spoon
4 ...... chopsticks
5 ...... cup
6 ...... glass
7 ...... plate
8 ...... bowl
9 ...... pepper
10 ...... salt
11 ...... sugar
12 ...... napkin

B 🔊 VB4.03 | Look at the photos again. Listen and repeat.

C Work in pairs. Cover the words in Ex 1B and discuss the questions.

1 What things in the photos are always on your table at breakfast?
2 What things do you have, but not on your table at home?
3 What things do you NOT have at home?

COMMUNICATION BANK

1B Ex 7 Student A

1 Look at the photos. Write three *yes/no* questions about photos D–F.

Photo D: Is he from the UK? Is he a singer? Is he an actor?

A

B

C

Chanda is from India. He's an office worker.

Anna is from Brazil. She's a music teacher.

It's the city of Krakow, in Poland.

D

E

F

2 Answer Student B's questions about photos A–C.

3 Ask Student B your questions about photos D–F.

2A Ex 7 Student A

1 Look at the photo and the information about three of your friends.

Names: Jamie, Mira, Keanu

Ages: all 24

Friends from university

Nationality: British, German, Brazilian

Where are they now? London

2 Cover the information and tell Student B about the people.

A: They're Jamie, Mira and …

3 Look at the photo of you and your friends. Choose one person to be you. Complete the information.

Names:

Ages:

Nationality:

Where are you now?

4 Cover the information and tell Student B about the people.

A: They're Luana, Demi and me. Luana is …

140

COMMUNICATION BANK   CB

8C Ex 6 Student A

1 You are a visitor to Mexico City in Mexico and you don't speak Spanish. You are at the bus station. It's 8.15 a.m. You want to buy a ticket to Toluca. Ask Student B questions to complete your notes.

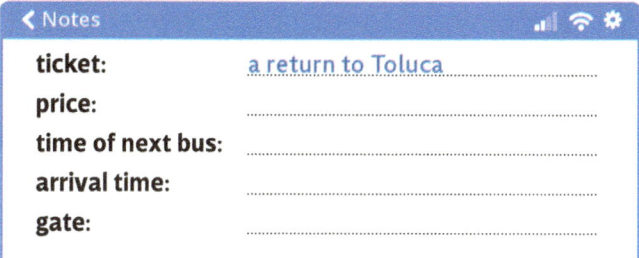

ticket:	a return to Toluca
price:	
time of next bus:	
arrival time:	
gate:	

2 You work at the train station in Poznań in Poland. Look at the information and answer Student B's questions.

Poznań to Warsaw: train service

Ticket prices: Single – €14 Return – €28
Times:

Departure	10:03	12:40	14:47
Arrival	13:17	16:28	18:26

Platform: 2

6A Ex 6 Student A

1 You can't find the things in the box. Ask Student B.

bag   camera   coat   guitar   laptop

A: Where's my bag?

2 Look at the picture and answer Student B's questions.

2A Ex 3C Student A

1 You are Jordan. Answer Student B's questions.

MEMBERSHIP CARD

Name	Jordan Browne
Age	37
Address	74 Plymouth Road
Email	jordanred88@coldmail.com

NOTICE   @ = 'at'   .com = 'dot com'

2 Student B is Pat. Ask questions and complete the information.

MEMBERSHIP CARD

Name	Pat
Age	
Address	
Email	

A: What's your name?
B: It's …
A: How do you spell that?

COMMUNICATION BANK

8C Ex 6 Student B

1 You work at the central bus station in Mexico City. Look at the information and answer Student A's questions.

Mexico City to Toluca: bus service

Ticket prices: Single – 70 pesos Return – 140 pesos
Times:

| Departure | 8:30 | 8:45 | 9:00 |
| Arrival | 10:00 | 10:15 | 10:30 |

Gate: 5

2 You are a tourist in Poznań in Poland and you don't speak Polish. You are at the train station. It's 8.30 a.m. You want to buy a ticket to Warsaw. Ask Student A questions to complete your notes.

‹ Notes

ticket: a return to Warsaw
price:
time of next train:
arrival time:
platform:

6A Ex 6 Student B

1 Look at the picture and answer Student A's questions.

2 You can't find the things in the box. Ask Student A.

| book   hat   headphones   shoe   umbrella |

B: Where's my book?

2A Ex 3C Student B

1 Student A is Jordan. Ask questions and complete the information.

MEMBERSHIP CARD

Name   Jordan
Age
Address
Email

B: What's your name?
A: It's …
B: How do you spell that?

2 You are Pat. Answer Student B's questions.

MEMBERSHIP CARD

Name   Pat Bourne
Age   29
Address 91 Hillside Street
Email   pat65@pb.co.uk

NOTICE   @ = 'at'   .co.uk = 'dot co dot uk'

COMMUNICATION BANK

1B Ex 7 Student B

1 Look at the photos. Write three *yes/no* questions about photos A–C.

Photo A: Is he Indian? Is he a teacher? Is he a student?

Marcus is from the UK. He's a police officer.

Paloma is from Spain. She's a businesswoman.

It's the city of Cape Town in South Africa.

2 Ask Student A your questions about photos A–C.

3 Answer Student A's questions about photos D–F.

2A Ex 7 Student B

1 Look at the photo and the information about three of your friends.

3 Look at the photo of you and your friends. Choose one person to be you. Complete the information.

Names: Sam, Cathy, Pete

Ages: 46, 25, 25

Friends from work

Nationality: British, Italian, Swiss

Where are they now? Italy

Names:

Ages:

Nationality:

Where are you now?

2 Cover the information and tell Student A about the people.

B: They're Sam, Cathy and …

4 Cover the information and tell Student A about the people.

B: They're Mark, Beatrice and me. Mark is …

COMMUNICATION BANK

3A Ex 6 Student A

Look at the picture. Then ask questions about Student B's picture. Find five differences.

A: In your picture, is Philip's bike red?
B: No, it's green. That's one difference! In your picture …

3B Ex 6B Student A

Look at the photo of your desk. Then ask Student B about the things on their desk. Find five things that are the same.

A: Do you have a computer?
B: No, I don't. I have a laptop. Do you have a … ?

6C Ex 5 Student A

Find the places in the box on your map. Ask Student B questions.

> a bus stop   a baker's
> a clothes shop
> a hospital   a hotel

A: Excuse me. Is there a bus stop near here?
B: Do you know the phone shop? Well, it's …

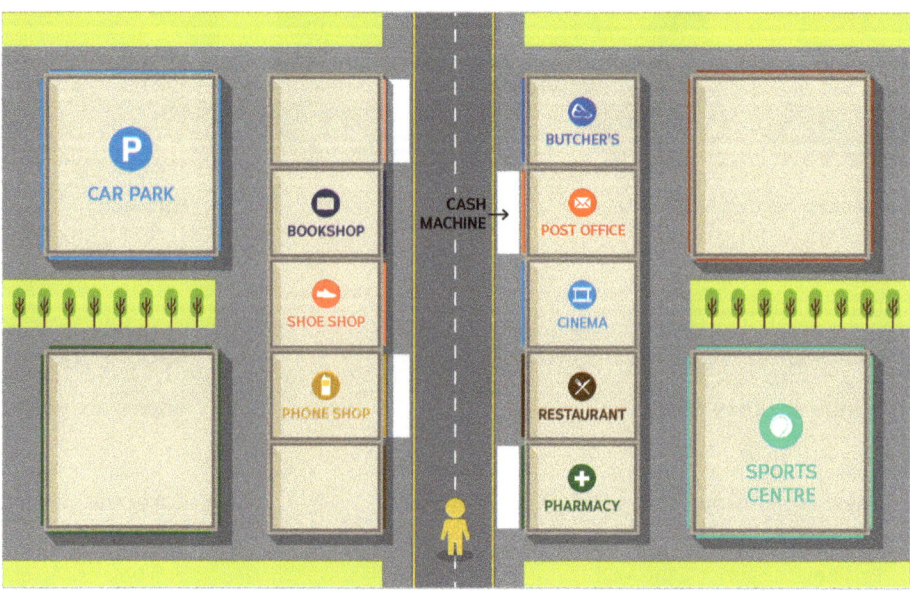

COMMUNICATION BANK

3C Ex 6 Student A

1 You're a customer in a market. Look at the pictures. Your favourite colour is black. You have €70. Ask Student B about the jackets.

A: Excuse me?
B: Yes? Can I help you?
A: Yes, how much … ?

2 You have a shop in a market. Look at the pictures. Answer Student B's questions.

You have …

B: Excuse me?
A: Yes? Can I help you?
B: Yes, how much … ?

4C Ex 6A Student B

1 Look at the café menu. You are the waiter. Take the customer's order. Ask questions.

B: Can I help you?
A: Yes, can I have a cup of coffee, please?
B: Espresso, latte or Americano?

2 Bring the customer's food and drink. Then respond to their requests.

3 Swap roles. Go back to page 43, Ex 6A.

5C Ex 5 Student B

Read the situations. Roleplay the conversations with Student A.

Situation 1

Student A is your manager and makes some requests. Give a polite answer.

- Of course.
- Sure.
- OK.
- All right.
- No problem.

Make offers

- get / a cup of coffee
  Can I get you a cup of coffee?
- get / sandwich

Situation 2

You are a passenger on a plane. Student A is a flight attendant. Make requests.

- help / bag   Can you help me with my bag?
- have / magazine
- have / bottle of water

Student A makes some offers. Give a polite answer.

- Yes, please.
- Thank you so much.
- No thanks, I'm fine.
- I'm OK, thanks.

1C Ex 6 Student A

Complete the table. Ask and answer questions with Student B.

	first name	surname	phone number
1	Misha		
2	Jean	Thibault	735 2245 63
3			
4	Katya	Kopp	745 5570 562

A: Number 1. What's your first name?
B: It's Misha.
A: How do you spell your first name?
B: M-I-S-H-A.

COMMUNICATION BANK

7B Ex 8 Student B

1 Read about Ellen MacArthur. Prepare questions to find the missing information in 1–6. Use the words in brackets to help you.

Ellen Macarthur, the famous sailor and businesswoman, is my hero.

1 She was born in ..1976.. in .... (When? Where?)
   B: **When was she born?**
   A: **She was born in 1976.**
2 When she was a child, her favourite place was .... with her aunt. (Where?)
3 She has the world record for sailing around the world alone. It was in 2005. She was .... (How old?)
4 She's retired now. She works with .... after their time in hospital. (Who?)
5 Her foundation, the .... Foundation, tries to find answers to world problems. (What?)
6 She's my hero because she's .... She's an amazing woman! (Why?)

2 Read about Giannis Antetokounmpo. Answer Student A's questions.

Giannis Antetokounmpo, the famous basketball player, is my hero.

1 He was born in Greece in 1994.
2 His parents were from Nigeria. His family was poor.
3 His parents were sportspeople. His father was a football player and his mother was a high jumper.
4 Now he plays in the USA in the NBA*.
5 His first NBA game was on 13 October, 2013. He was eighteen years old.
6 He's my hero because he's strong and fast and he's amazing to watch.

*National Basketball Association

3 Ask your questions. Remember to use question words to check you understand.
   B: **When was she born?**
   A: **She was born in 1976.**
   B: **Sorry, when?**

COMMUNICATION BANK

CB

3A Ex 6 Student B

Look at the picture. Then ask questions about Student A's picture. Find five differences.

B: In your picture, is Philip's bike green?
A: No, it's red. That's one difference! In your picture …

3B Ex 6B Student B

Look at the photo of your desk. Then ask Student A about the things on their desk. Find five things that are the same.

B: Do you have headphones?
A: No, I don't. Do you have a … ?

6C Ex 5 Student B

Find the places in the box on your map. Ask Student A questions.

> a bookshop   a car park
> a cash machine
> a restaurant
> a sports centre

B: Excuse me. Is there a bookshop near here?
A: Do you know the post office? Well, it's …

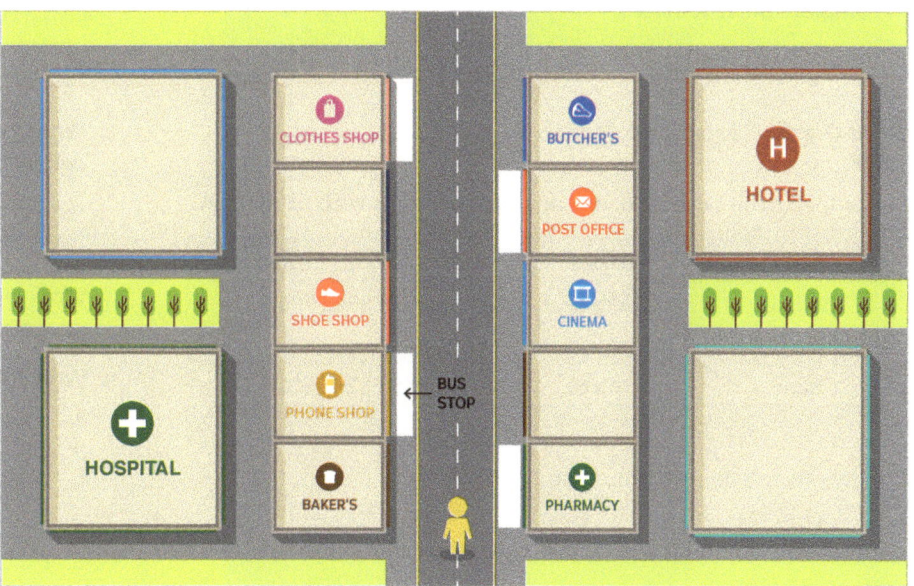

147

COMMUNICATION BANK

3C Ex 6 Student B

1 You have a shop in a market. Look at the pictures. Answer Student A's questions.

You have …

A: Excuse me?
B: Yes? Can I help you?
A: Yes, how much … ?

2 You're a customer in a market. Look at the pictures. Your favourite colour is blue. You have €35. Ask Student A about the jumpers.

B: Excuse me?
A: Yes? Can I help you?
B: Yes, how much … ?

2B Ex 7A Student B

1 Write questions with *How old*, *Where* and *What* to find the missing information (1–7) in the text.

1 How old is Keith?

Keith McKenny, ¹............ (age), and Filipa Zampa, forty-five, are husband and wife. Filipa is Italian and Keith is from ²............ (country). Their home is in the USA, but their children are in ³............ (place). Their daughter Zoe is twenty-five, and she's in ⁴............ (country). She's a manager at a hotel in ⁵............ (city). Their son Andreas is ⁶............ (age) and he's in Italy. He's a ⁷............ (job) at a restaurant in Rome.

2 Answer Student A's questions. Then ask the questions to complete the text in Ex 1.

1C Ex 6 Student B

Complete the table. Ask and answer questions with Student A.

	first name	surname	phone number
1	Misha	Sergeeva	915 8642 705
2			
3	Elias	Chiasa	40 532 6260
4			

A: Number 1. What's your first name?
B: It's Misha.
A: How do you spell your first name?
B: M-I-S-H-A.

5A Ex 3A Student B

A good colleague …

- starts work at nine o'clock and leaves at five (in a 9–5 job).
- says 'good morning' with a smile
- doesn't take a two-hour lunch break.
- listens to their colleagues.
- sometimes gets coffee for people.
- doesn't call friends in work time.
- doesn't forget important dates, for example birthdays.
- thanks people for their help.
- never sends work emails at the weekend.
- helps people with their work problems.

1 Read the text about Claudia. Then look at the list above. Which points are true for Claudia?

My colleague, Claudia

I work in a small company. Claudia is a good colleague. She's friendly and I really like her. She's a good worker. She always starts work at nine and she never leaves first. She often says something nice about my clothes – 'Nice dress!' or 'Great jacket!' She doesn't call friends in work time (other people often speak to their friends in work time – I hate it!). She never forgets other people's birthdays and she always gets them something nice. And she never sends us emails at the weekend.

Claudia's not perfect. She helps me with my work problems (and that's a good thing) and I thank her. But sometimes I help her with work and she doesn't often say thank you. It's not a big problem, just a bit strange.

2 Write five questions about Student A's colleague, René. Use the list above to help you.

Does he start work at nine?
Does he call friends in work time?

3 Work in pairs and take turns. Ask and answer your questions.

4 Work in pairs and discuss the questions.
  1 What is the same about Claudia and René?
  2 Which person is the best colleague? Why?

COMMUNICATION BANK

7B Ex 8 Student A

1 Read about Giannis Antetokounmpo. Prepare questions to find the missing information in 1–6. Use the words in brackets to help you.

Giannis Antetokounmpo, the famous basketball player, is my hero.
1 He was born in *Greece* in .... (Where? When?)
   A: Where was he born?
   B: He was born in Greece.
2 His parents were from .... and his family was poor. (Where?)
3 His parents were sportspeople. His father was a .... and his mother was a high jumper. (What / father's / sport?)
4 Now he plays in .... in the NBA*. (Where?)
5 His first NBA game was on 13 October .... He was eighteen years old. (What year?)
6 He's my hero because he's .... and he's amazing to watch. (Why?)

*National Basketball Association

2 Ask your questions. Remember to use question words to check you understand.
   A: Where was he born?
   B: He was born in Greece.
   A: Sorry, where?

3 Read about Ellen MacArthur. Answer Student B's questions.

Ellen MacArthur, the famous sailor and businesswoman, is my hero.
1 She was born in England in 1976.
2 When she was a child, her favourite place was on a boat with her aunt.
3 She has the world record for sailing around the world alone. It was in 2005. She was twenty-eight.
4 She's retired now. She works with young people after their time in hospital.
5 Her foundation, the Ellen MacArthur Foundation, tries to find answers to world problems.
6 She's my hero because she's strong and positive. She's an amazing woman.

COMMUNICATION BANK

2D Ex 2A

1 Work in pairs. Look at the photos (A–G). Choose the best three cakes.

I like Oli's cake.
Me too. And I like Elisabetta's cake.
Elisabetta's cake is beautiful.

2 Who are your three winners? Write their names.

Elisabetta's cake

Suzie's cake

Oli's cake

Sarah's cake

Robin's cake

Georgia's cake

Katie's cake

SOUNDS AND SPELLING   SSp

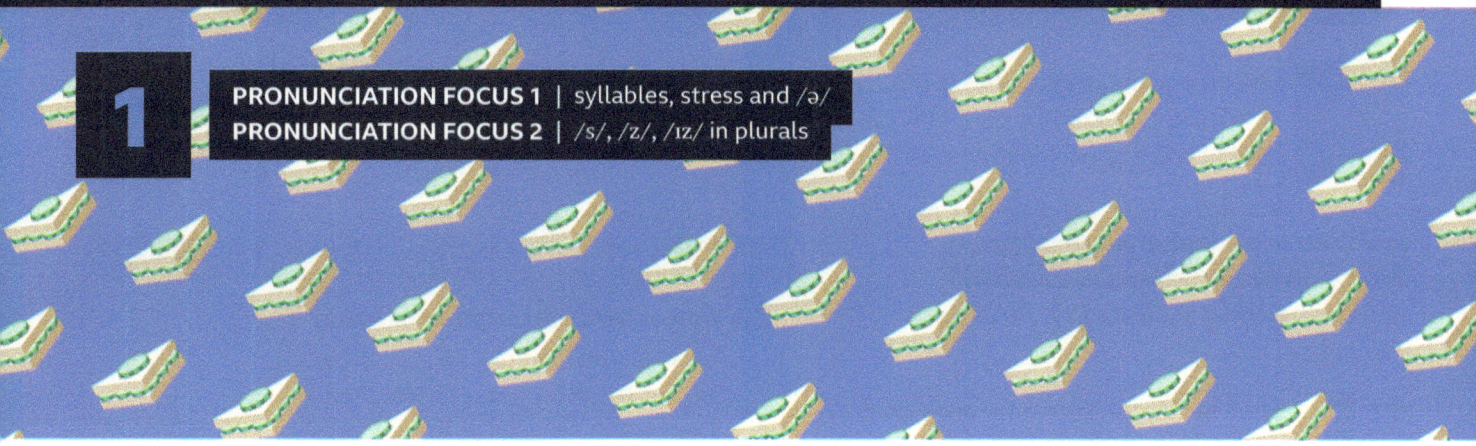

1 PRONUNCIATION FOCUS 1 | syllables, stress and /ə/
      PRONUNCIATION FOCUS 2 | /s/, /z/, /ɪz/ in plurals

PRONUNCIATION FOCUS 1

syllables, stress and /ə/

1 A Work in pairs. Read the tip. Then complete the table with the words in the box.

> **PRONUNCIATION TIP** ✓
>
> Words have parts called syllables. A syllable has one vowel sound. *Bus* has one syllable, *doctor* has two syllables, *computer* has three syllables.

| afternoon | digital | four | internet | night |
| number | pizza | sandwich | singer | Spain |

(afternoon is crossed out)

one syllable	two syllables	three syllables
bus	doctor	computer
		afternoon

B S1.01 | Listen and check. Then listen again and repeat.

2 S1.02 | Read the tip. Then listen to words from Ex 1A. Underline the stressed syllable.

> **PRONUNCIATION TIP** ✓
>
> One syllable in the word is stressed.
>
> It is l o n g, LOUD and ^high^.
>
> do<u>c</u>tor, com<u>pu</u>ter

3 S1.03 | Read the tip. Then listen and repeat the sound and the words.

> **PRONUNCIATION TIP** ✓
>
> The schwa /ə/ sound is weak and is in unstressed syllables.
>
> tea**ch**er, **do**ctor, A**me**rica
>   /ə/   /ə/ /ə/   /ə/

1 teach**er**, comput**er**
2 doct**or**, inf**or**mation
3 **A**meric**a**, shop **a**ssist**a**nt
4 list**e**n, stud**e**nt

4 A Work in pairs. Look at the words in Ex 3 again and complete the tip.

> **SPELLING TIP** ✓
>
> In words we often spell /ə/:
>
> 1 er
> 2 ....
> 3 ....
> 4 ....

B Work in pairs. Complete the words.

1 He's a wait**er**.
2 She's sev......n.
3 It's in Pol......nd.
4 Good aft......noon.
5 Answ...... the question.
6 Just ...... mom......nt.
7 It's from Br......zil.
8 I'm a sing...... .
9 No probl......m.
10 He's ......n act...... .
11 It's in Chin...... .
12 I don't und......stand.

C 🔊 S1.04 | Listen and repeat.

PRONUNCIATION FOCUS 2

/s/, /z/, /ɪz/ in plurals

5 A Work in pairs. What are the plural forms of the words in the circles?

B 🔊 S1.05 | Listen and match the plural endings (A–C) in Ex 5A with the sounds: /s/, /z/ and /ɪz/.

C 🔊 S1.05 | Listen again and repeat.

SOUNDS AND SPELLING

2
PRONUNCIATION FOCUS 1 | short and long sounds (1): /ɪ/, /iː/, /ʊ/, /uː/
PRONUNCIATION FOCUS 2 | /w/ and /h/ in question words
SPELLING | special spellings /ɪ/, /iː/, /ʊ/ and /uː/

PRONUNCIATION FOCUS 1

short and long sounds (1): /ɪ/, /iː/, /ʊ/, /uː/

1 A **S2.01** | Read the tip. Then listen and repeat the sounds and the words.

PRONUNCIATION TIP ✓
English vowel sounds are short or **l o n g**.
/ɪ/ and /ʊ/ are short; /iː/ and /uː/ are long.

/ɪ/ **i**t, s**i**x, ch**i**ldren, **E**nglish, **e**leven
/iː/ eight**ee**n, ninet**ee**n, **ea**sy, t**ea**cher, **e**mail
/ʊ/ g**oo**d, b**oo**k, f**oo**tball, l**oo**k, difficult
/uː/ aftern**oo**n, ch**oo**se, **U**K, **u**niversity, tr**ue**

B Look at the words in Ex 1A again and complete the tip.

SPELLING TIP ✓
In words we often spell:
/ɪ/	1 i_____	2 _____	
/iː/	1 _____	2 _____	3 _____
/ʊ/	1 _____	2 _____	
/uː/	1 _____	2 _____	3 _____

C 🔊 **S2.02** | Listen and match what you hear with the correct word (a–d).

 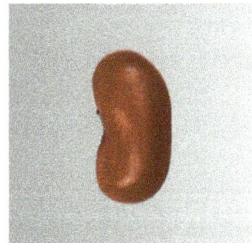

a bin 1, **b** bean

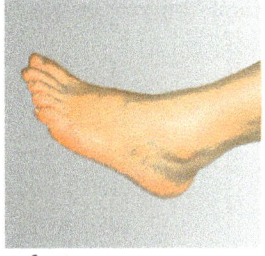 

c foot **d** food

D Work in pairs. Student A: Say a word from Ex 1C. Student B: Point to the correct photo.

SPECIAL SPELLINGS

2 A Work in pairs and complete the words.

1 a b**u**sinessman /ɪ/
2 three p__ple
3 just a min_te
4 How are y__?
5 a pol_ce officer
6 t__ sisters
7 a w_man
8 six w_m_n
9 a n__ car
10 It's b___tiful.

B Work in pairs. Match the spellings (1–10) in Ex 2A with the sounds: /ɪ/, /iː/, /ʊ/ and /uː/.

C **S2.03** | Listen and check. Then listen again and repeat.

3 Read the tip. Then choose five words in bold from Ex 2A and write the correct sound under each difficult spelling.

PRONUNCIATION TIP ✓
Some English spellings are difficult to pronounce. Write the sound under a difficult spelling, to help you remember the pronunciation.

b**u**sinessman
/ɪ/

4 🔊 **S2.04** | Listen and find two examples of each sound in the sentences.

1 I'm Kim. I'm twenty-three. I'm a police officer.
/ɪ/ Kim _____
/iː/ _____ _____

2 I'm forty-two. I'm a bus driver in the UK. It's a difficult job, but it's good.
/ʊ/ _____ _____
/uː/ _____ _____

PRONUNCIATION FOCUS 2

/w/ and /h/ in question words

5 A Complete the question words.

1 __at's your name?
2 __ere are you from?
3 __en is your English class?
4 __o's your teacher?
5 _ow do you spell your name?

B Complete the table with the question words in Ex 5A.

/w/	/h/
What	

C 🔊 **S2.05** | Listen and check. Then listen again and repeat.

D Work in pairs. Ask and answer the questions in Ex 5A.

SOUNDS AND SPELLING

SSp

3 | PRONUNCIATION FOCUS 1 | voiced and unvoiced consonants (1): /p/ and /b/, /k/ and /g/, /t/ and /d/
PRONUNCIATION FOCUS 2 | sounds at the end of words

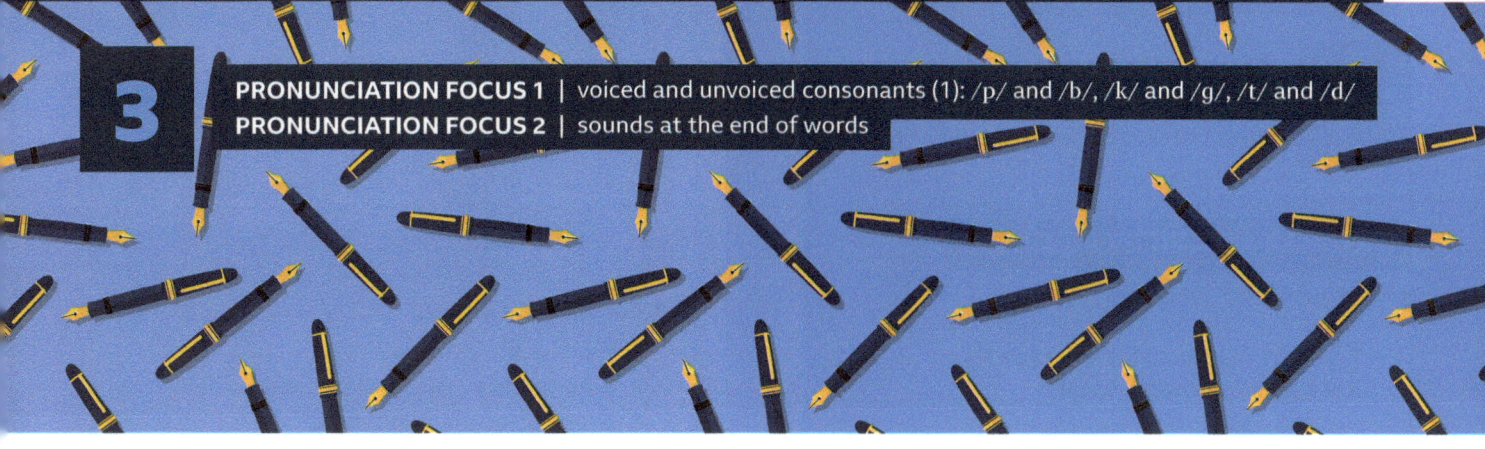

PRONUNCIATION FOCUS 1

voiced and unvoiced consonants (1): /p/ and /b/, /k/ and /g/, /t/ and /d/

1 A 🔊 **S3.01** | Read the tip. Then listen and repeat the sounds and the words.

> **PRONUNCIATION TIP** ✓
>
> We use our voice for some consonants, e.g. /b/, /g/ and /d/.
>
> We don't use our voice for other consonants, e.g. /p/, /k/ and /t/.

/p/ **p**en, **p**eople, ha**pp**y, cu**p**, sho**p**
/b/ **b**ank, **b**ed, **b**a**b**y, we**b**site, jo**b**
/k/ **c**amera, **c**offee, ja**ck**et, bla**ck**, thin**k**
/g/ **g**irl, **g**oodbye, **gu**itar, bi**g**, ba**g**
/t/ **T**-shirt, wai**t**er, le**tt**er, sui**t**, wha**t**
/d/ **d**octor, **d**ark, a**dd**ress, re**d**, ba**d**

B Look at the words in Ex 1A again and complete the tip.

> **SPELLING TIP** ✓
>
> In words we spell:
> /p/   1 p........   2 ....
> /b/   1 ....
> /k/   1 ....   2 ....   3 ....
> /g/   1 ....   2 ....
> /t/   1 ....   2 ....
> /d/   1 ....   2 ....
>
> We pronounce a double letter (*pp*, *dd*) the same as a single letter (*p*, *d*).

2 A 🔊 **S3.02** | Listen and match with the correct word or phrase (a–f).

a It's a pea. 1,   b It's a bee. 2, 3

c It's cold.   d It's gold.

e town   f down

B Work in pairs. Student A: Say a word or phrase from Ex 2A. Student B: Point to the correct photo.

PRONUNCIATION FOCUS 2

sounds at the end of words

3 A 🔊 **S3.03** | Read the tip. Then listen and repeat the phrases and sentences (1–8).

> **PRONUNCIATION TIP** ✓
>
> We link a word ending with a consonant sound (*cup, what*) to a word beginning with a vowel sound (*of, are*). It's important to pronounce the final consonant: *cup of, what are*.

1 cup	cup of	a cup of coffee
2 job	job in	a job in town
3 think	think it's	I think it's great.
4 bag	bag of	a bag of bananas
5 what	What are	What are your names?
6 good	good answer	a good answer
7 love	love it	I love it.
8 like	like it	I don't like it.

B Work in pairs. Practise saying the phrases and sentences.

153

SOUNDS AND SPELLING

PRONUNCIATION FOCUS 1 | short vowels: /e/, /æ/, /ʌ/
PRONUNCIATION FOCUS 2 | *does*: /dʌz/ or /dəz/?
SPELLING | special spellings /ʌ/ and /e/

PRONUNCIATION FOCUS 1
short vowels: /e/, /æ/, /ʌ/

1 A **S4.01** | Listen to the short vowels /e/, /æ/ and /ʌ/. Then listen again and repeat.

/e/ **e**gg, p**e**pper, g**e**t, n**e**ver, tw**e**lve
/æ/ **a**pple, c**a**rrot, n**a**pkin, h**a**t, **A**frica
/ʌ/ m**u**shroom, l**u**nch, s**o**metimes, l**o**ve, m**o**ther

B Work in pairs. Look at the words in Ex 1A again and complete the tip.

> **SPELLING TIP** ✓
> In words we usually spell:
> /e/   1 e............
> /æ/   1 ....
> /ʌ/   1 ....   2 ....

2 A **S4.02** | Look at the photos and listen to the words. Then listen again and repeat.

1 c**a**p /æ/

c**u**p /ʌ/

2 h**a**t /æ/

h**u**t /ʌ/

3 m**a**n /æ/

m**e**n /e/

B **S4.03** | Listen and find the words. Go up (↑) or down (↓), left (←) or right (→).

START		
cap ↓	cap	cup
cup	hat	men
hut	cup	man
hat	men	cap
man	hut	hut
men	hat	hat
		FINISH

C Work in pairs. Student A: Say a word from Ex 2A. Student B: Point to the correct word.

SPECIAL SPELLINGS

3 A Complete the words.
1 We have **br_ _kfast** at seven.
2 Nate is very **y_ _ng**, only two years old.
3 Where are my **h_ _dphones**?
4 That's my **fr_ _nd** Amy.
5 It's **_n_** o'clock.
6 Do you have **_ny** eggs?
7 Can you say it **ag_ _n**, please?
8 In my **c_ _ntry**, we speak Spanish.

B **S4.04** | Listen to the words and sentences in Ex 3A. Then listen again and repeat.

C Write the words in bold in Ex 3A and the correct sound under each difficult spelling.

br**ea**kfast
  /e/

PRONUNCIATION FOCUS 2
***does*: /dʌz/ or /dəz/?**

4 A Underline the stressed words in the conversation.
A: Does your <u>classroom</u> have a <u>computer</u>?
B: Yes, it does.
A: Does it have a blackboard?
B: No, it doesn't. It has a whiteboard.

B **S4.05** | Work in pairs. Match *does* in Ex 4A with the correct sound: /dʌz/ or /dəz/. Then listen and check.

C Work in pairs. Choose the correct words to complete the tip.

> **PRONUNCIATION TIP** ✓
> When we **stress / don't stress** *does*, it's /dəz/.
> When we **stress / don't stress** *does*, it's /dʌz/.
> *Doesn't* is always /dʌzənt/.

5 A Write two colours, two types of clothes and two types of food or drink.

B Work in pairs and take turns. Ask the questions (1–3) about spelling. Guess your partner's words.
1 Does it start with … ?
2 Does it finish with … ?
3 Does it have … letters?

A: It's a colour.
B: Does it start with Y?
A: No, it doesn't.

PRONUNCIATION SOUND CHART

VOWEL SOUNDS

■ = short vowels   ■ = long vowels   ■ = diphthongs

ə doctor /ˈdɒktə/	ɜː shirt /ʃɜːt/	ɪ fish /fɪʃ/	iː bee /biː/
ʊ book /bʊk/	uː shoe /ʃuː/	æ match /mætʃ/	ɑː car /kɑː/
ɒ clock /klɒk/	ɔː horse /hɔːs/	e egg /eg/	ʌ cup /kʌp/
aɪ bike /baɪk/	eɪ cake /keɪk/	əʊ coat /kəʊt/	eə chair /tʃeə/
ɪə earring /ˈɪərɪŋ/	ɔɪ boy /bɔɪ/	aʊ cow /kaʊ/	ʊə tourist /ˈtʊərɪst/

CONSONANT SOUNDS

■ = unvoiced   ■ = voiced

p pen /pen/	b book /bʊk/	t tea /tiː/	d dog /dɒg/
k cat /kæt/	g girl /gɜːl/	s sun /sʌn/	z zebra /ˈzebrə/
θ earth /ɜːθ/	ð mother /ˈmʌðə/	ʃ sheep /ʃiːp/	ʒ television /ˈtelɪˌvɪʒən/
f flower /ˈflaʊə/	v van /væn/	tʃ cheese /tʃiːz/	dʒ jeans /dʒiːnz/
m man /mæn/	n nut /nʌt/	ŋ king /kɪŋ/	h hat /hæt/
l lamp /læmp/	r ring /rɪŋ/	w woman /ˈwʊmən/	j yacht /jɒt/

AUDIOSCRIPTS

LEAD-IN

Audio L.01
A   a restaurant
B   a photo
C   a pizza
D   a park
E   a coffee
F   a bus

Audio L.02
zero, one, two, three, four, five, six, seven, eight, nine, ten

Audio L.03
five, nine, one, seven, ten, zero, six, three, eight, two, four

Audio L.04
Monday, Tuesday, Wednesday, Thursday, Friday, Saturday, Sunday

Audio L.05
L = Lin   F = Franco   J = Jo   S = Stefan
L: Franco, what's 'lápiz' in English?
F: I don't know.
L: Jo, what's 'lápiz' in English?
J: It's a pencil.
L: Thank you!

J: It's on page nine.
S: I don't understand. Can you repeat that, please?
J: Yes. Page nine. The page in the book. Six, seven, eight, nine …
S: OK, I understand. Thank you.

LEAD-IN VOCABULARY BANK

Audio VB.L.01
A   a phone
B   a camera
C   a passport
D   a menu
E   a taxi
F   a hotel
G   a computer
H   a university
I   a bank
J   a supermarket

Audio VB.L.02
A   listen
B   look at
C   ask
D   answer
E   work alone
F   say 'hello'
G   read
H   match
I   work in pairs
J   write
K   choose
L   check your answers

UNIT 1

Audio 1.01
J = James   S = Sonia
Conversation 1
J: Erm, hi.
S: Hello.
J: Are you a student?
S: Yes, I am. Are you?
J: Yes, I am. What's your name?
S: I'm Sonia.
J: I'm James. Nice to meet you.
S: Nice to meet you, too. Where are you from, James?
J: I'm from Canada.
S: Oh, where in Canada?
J: From Vancouver. And you, Sonia?
S: I'm from the UK, from Manchester.

A = Anna   J = Jack
Conversation 2
A: Good morning, everyone. Today, Jack Brown is with us. Jack?
J: Hi, everyone. I'm Jack, Jack Brown.
A: Good morning, Jack.
J: I'm in China. So for me it's 'good afternoon'.
A: Are you in Beijing?
J: No, today I'm in Shanghai.
A: So, let's go round the table and …

Audio 1.02
S = Shanaya   B = Ben
S: Hello, I'm Shanaya.
B: Hi, Shanaya, I'm Ben. Nice to meet you.
S: You too. Where are you from, Ben?
B: I'm from Germany.
S: Oh, where in Germany?
B: From Berlin.
S: Are you a student here?
B: Yes, I am. Are you from the UK, Shanaya?
S: No, I'm not. I'm from India.

Audio 1.03
A: Hello, I'm Sonia.
B: Hi, Sonia. I'm James. Nice to meet you.

Audio 1.04
1   a doctor
2   a teacher
3   a waiter
4   a taxi driver
5   a singer

Audio 1.05
A, B, C, D, E, F, G, H, I, J, K, L, M, N, O, P, Q, R, S, T, U, V, W, X, Y, Z

Audio 1.06
1   A H J K
2   B C D E G P T V
3   F L M N S X Z
4   I Y
5   O
6   Q U W
7   R

Audio 1.07
Conversation 1
A: Can I help you?
B: Yes. I'm here for the conference.
A: What's your name?
B: Imogen Menzie.
A: How do you spell your surname?
B: M-E-N-Z-I-E
A: OK, here it is. First name Imogen?
B: That's right. I-M-O-G-E-N.
A: Here's your name card. The conference is in room 238.
B: Thank you. Oh wait, there's a mistake …

Conversation 2
C: Hello.
D: Hello. I'm a new student.
C: OK. What's your name?
D: Eduardo Lopez.
C: How do you spell your surname?
D: L-O-P-E-Z.
C: Just a moment. L-O-P-A-Z?
D: No, L-O-P-E-Z.
C: Sorry, L-O-P-E-Z?
D: Perfect.
C: And your first name … E-D-U-A-R-D-O… ?
D: That's right.
C: Great. And what's your phone number?
D: It's 9-1-3-8-4-5-6-6-0.
C: Sorry, can you repeat that, please?
D: 9-1-3-8-4-5-6-6-0.
C: OK, Eduardo. Here's your student card.
D: Thank you!
C: No problem.

Conversation 3
E: What's your surname?
F: It's Clarke.
E: Clarke … Hmm … How do you spell that?
F: C-L-A-R-K-E.
E: Your name isn't here.
F: Really?
E: What's your first name?
F: Amelia.
E: Amelia Clarke. Just a moment … Ah, here it is.
F: Oh good.
E: Erm, what's your phone number?
F: It's 3-2-8-6-3-2-8.
E: Sorry, 3-2-8-6-3-8-2?
F: 2-8.
E: OK, 3-2-8-6-3-2-8.
F: Yes.
E: OK, great, thank you. Here's your key card. You're in room 729.
F: Thank you. Oh wait, there's a mistake …

Audio 1.08
1   A: What's your name?
    B: Imogen Menzie.
2   A: How do you spell your surname?
    B: M-E-N-Z-I-E.
3   A: Great. And what's your phone number?
    B: It's 9-1-3-8-4-5-6-6-0.
    A: Sorry, can you repeat that, please?
4   A: What's your surname?
    B: It's Clarke.
5   A: What's your first name?
    B: Amelia.

AUDIOSCRIPTS

UNIT 1 VOCABULARY BANK

Audio VB1.01
Argentina, Argentinian
Australia, Australian
Brazil, Brazilian
Colombia, Colombian
India, Indian
Italy, Italian
Mexico, Mexican
the US, the USA, American
South Africa, South African
South Korea, South Korean
Poland, Polish
Spain, Spanish
Turkey, Turkish
the UK, British
China, Chinese
Vietnam, Vietnamese
Japan, Japanese
France, French
Germany, German
Switzerland, Swiss

Audio VB1.02
A football player
B bus driver
C businessman, businesswoman
D artist
E shop assistant
F nurse
G actor
H police officer
I office worker
J digital designer

Audio VB1.03
1 a bus driver
2 an actor
3 a nurse
4 a police officer
5 a shop assistant
6 an office worker
7 a businessman, a businesswoman
8 a digital designer
9 a football player
10 an artist

Audio VB1.04
A sandwich
B bag
C bottle of water
D purse
E key
F laptop
G notebook
H banana
I mobile phone
J umbrella
K wallet
L make-up
M book

UNIT 1 REVIEW

Audio R1.01
English fun facts
The top (number 1) letter in English is 'e'. The top adjective is 'good' and the top noun is 'time'. The top words are 'I' and 'you'. The English alphabet has five vowels: a, e, i, o and u. Greek has seven vowels and the Polish alphabet has nine vowels. English has many words from other languages. 'Zero' is from Arabic, 'guitar' is from Spanish and 'shampoo' is from the Indian language Hindi. 'Café' and 'art' are from French. English numbers have difficult spellings! '1' isn't 'wun', it's 'one'; '2' isn't 'too', it's 'two'; and '8' is 'eight'. Crazy!

UNIT 1 SOUNDS AND SPELLING

Audio S1.01
one syllable: bus, four, night, Spain
two syllables: doctor, number, pizza, sandwich, singer
three syllables: computer, afternoon, digital, internet

Audio S1.02
1 doctor
2 number
3 pizza
4 singer
5 computer
6 afternoon
7 digital
8 internet

Audio S1.03
/ə/, /ə/
1 teacher, computer
2 doctor, information
3 America, shop assistant
4 listen, student

Audio S1.04
1 He's a waiter.
2 She's seven.
3 It's in Poland.
4 Good afternoon.
5 Answer the question.
6 Just a moment.
7 It's from Brazil.
8 I'm a singer.
9 No problem.
10 He's an actor.
11 It's in China.
12 I don't understand.

Audio S1.05
names, emails, keys
books, passports, shops
boxes, buses, sandwiches

UNIT 2

Audio 2.01
eleven, twelve, thirteen, fourteen, fifteen, sixteen, seventeen, eighteen, nineteen, twenty

Audio 2.02
thirty, forty, fifty, sixty, seventy, eighty, ninety, a hundred

Audio 2.03
thirteen, thirty
fourteen, forty
fifteen, fifty
sixteen, sixty
seventeen, seventy
eighteen, eighty
nineteen, ninety

Audio 2.04
brother, brother
sister, sister
husband, husband
wife, wife
parents, parents
children, children
father, father
daughter, daughter
mother, mother
son, son

Audio 2.05
My name's Mark. I'm American, and I'm from New York City, and my family … Well, it's a very international family. I have a sister in France, a brother in Colombia, and our parents are in New York. I'm in Italy, and I have a beautiful daughter, Mia. She's eight and she's a student at school here.
My sister Jessica and her husband Thomas are in France. They have a restaurant in Paris. Jessica's forty-five. She's a good mother, and she's a great sister to me. Their children are in the UK, in London. Their son, Justin, is twenty-one now. He's a writer for a magazine. I don't remember its name. Their daughter Emma is eighteen and she's a student at university.
My brother David and his family are in Colombia. David's thirty-eight. His wife, Mariana, is Colombian. They have two young children, Antonella and Matías. David's a doctor. He often says 'Come and visit! It's perfect for your holiday!' But they're in Colombia and I'm in Italy! We're very happy in Italy, but we really are an international family!

Audio 2.06
D = Dave   J = Jen   K = Katie
N = Nick   A = Andy   S = Susanna
Conversation 1
D: Hey, Jen, how are you?
J: Hi, Dave. Not bad, thanks. Coffee?
D: Yes, please. Black with sugar.
J: Here.
D: Thanks.
J: How are you?
D: Good, thanks. How's work?
J: It's OK. How are your children?
D: They're great, thanks. Lena's three now and Stella's six. I have a photo.
J: Aw … They're beautiful!
D: Yes … Oh, look at the time! Thanks for the coffee.
J: No problem.

Conversation 2
K: Hi, Nick.
N: Hey, Katie. Are you OK?
K: Yes, great. You?
N: Good, thanks. It's a beautiful day.
K: Yes, it is. How's your new car?
N: It's really good. We're very happy with it.
K: Great!
N: I'm really hot … and tired.
K: Me too. Ah here's my street. See you.
N: See you later! Say 'hello' to Greg!

Conversation 3
A: Hey, Susanna! Where's our class?
S: Hi! Er … Anthony?
A: Andy.

AUDIOSCRIPTS

S: Sorry, Andy. Our class? Just a moment. It's 617. Yeah, room 617.
A: How are you?
S: Very well, thanks. You?
A: I'm fine.
S: Hey, Andy, you have art classes, right?
A: That's right.
S: How's your new teacher? Ms Brown?
A: She's really good and she's very friendly.
S: Oh that's good. Ah, here we are, room 617.

Audio 2.07
D = Dave   J = Jen   N = Nick   K = Katie
S = Susanna   A = Andy
Conversation 1
D: Hey, Jen, how are you?
J: Hi, Dave. Not bad, thanks. Coffee?
D: Yes, please. Black with sugar. How's work?
J: It's OK. How are your children?
D: They're great, thanks. Oh, look at the time! Thanks for the coffee.
J: No problem.

Conversation 2
N: It's a beautiful day.
K: Yes, it is. How's your new car?
N: It's really good. We're very happy with it.
K: Great!
N: I'm really hot ... and tired.
K: Me too. Ah, here's my street. See you.
N: See you later! Say 'hello' to Greg!

Conversation 3
S: How's your new teacher? Ms Brown?
A: She's really good and she's very friendly.

Audio 2.08
1 It's a beautiful day.
2 No problem.
3 How's your new car?
4 Me too.

Audio 2.09
A: Who's Judi?
B: Judi's my sister. I have a photo.
A: Nice photo! How old is she?
B: She's thirty.
A: And who's Dennis?
B: He's a good friend.
A: Where's he from?
B: He's from Singapore.
A: Is he married?
B: Yes, he is. He has a wife and a daughter.
A: Who's Kenji?
B: Kenji is someone from work.
A: Where's Kenji from?
B: He's Japanese. He's from Tokyo.
A: What's his job?
B: He's a sales assistant in our shop. He's really nice.

UNIT 2 VOCABULARY BANK

Audio VB2.01
A young, old
B hot, cold
C friendly
D new, old
E beautiful
F good, bad
G favourite
H tired
I happy, sad
J big, small
K easy, difficult

Audio VB2.02
A girl
B friend
C man
D person
E baby
F child
G boy
H woman

Audio VB2.03
1 people, person
2 men, man
3 women, woman
4 children, child

UNIT 2 REVIEW

Audio R2.01
A family business
Burger24/7 is a hamburger restaurant in Adelaide, Australia. Tom, the manager, says, 'We're all family here. My mother is here from 10 o'clock in the morning. My son and daughter are at school, but they're in the restaurant at weekends.' Tom's wife is also in the family business. She's Samantha, and she's the head chef. 'People ask us, "Why are you open 24/7?"' says Samantha. 'Well, we're open 24/7 because people are hungry 24/7.' Samantha has a brother, but he's not in the family business. 'He says we're crazy. He asks me, "Samantha, what are your summer holiday plans?"' Samantha says, 'What holiday? Our restaurant is our life!'

UNIT 2 SOUNDS AND SPELLING

Audio S2.01
/ɪ/   it, six, children, English, eleven
/iː/ eighteen, nineteen, easy, teacher, email
/ʊ/   good, book, football, look, difficult
/uː/ afternoon, choose, UK, university, true

Audio S2.02
1 bin
2 bean
3 bin
4 bin
5 bean
6 bean
7 bean
8 bin
9 bin
10 bean
11 foot
12 food
13 food
14 foot
15 foot
16 foot
17 food
18 food
19 foot
20 food

Audio S2.03
1 a businessman
2 three people
3 just a minute
4 How are you?
5 a police officer
6 two sisters
7 a woman
8 six women
9 a new car
10 It's beautiful.

Audio S2.04
1 I'm Kim. I'm twenty-three. I'm a police officer.
2 I'm forty-two. I'm a bus driver in the UK. It's a difficult job, but it's good.

Audio S2.05
/w/
What, What
What's your name?
Where, Where
Where are you from?
When, When
When is your English class?
/h/
Who, Who
Who's your teacher?
How, How
How do you spell your name?

UNIT 3

Audio 3.01
1 my grandmother's ring
2 Pat's guitar
3 Alice's watch
4 my father's camera

Audio 3.02
/s/   Philip's phone, Irmak's guitar
/z/   Susan's bag, Carol's book
/ɪz/ Felix's camera, Darsh's bike

Audio 3.03
TW = Toni White   S = Sandy   J = Joe
TW: Hello, this is Toni White. Welcome to ... *We're all Different!* Today is about people and their desks. What do people have on their desks? How are the desks different? First of all, Sandy. Are you there?
S: Hi, yes, I'm here.
TW: Sandy, do you have a job?
S: No, I don't. I'm a student at college. I'm an art student.
TW: OK, so Sandy, what's on your desk?
S: Well, my desk is small and I have a lot of things on it. I have a computer and a keyboard ... a mouse ... and ... a notebook and a pen. I have a cup of coffee. I also have some sticky notes ... scissors ... my glasses ...
TW: Do you have any pencils? For your artwork?
S: No, I don't have any pencils on my desk.
TW: So, what's different about your desk?
S: Different?
TW: Yes, different. I mean, everybody has a computer, a mouse, scissors ...

AUDIOSCRIPTS

S: Oh, I see. OK. Well, I have three plants. And oh, my pens are in a cup, a blue cup from Paris.
TW: Very nice. Thank you, Sandy!
S: You're welcome.
TW: And next is Joe. Joe, do you have a job?
J: Yes, I do. I'm a digital designer.
TW: And what do you have on your desk, Joe?
J: Well, of course I have a computer and a keyboard. What else? I have a notebook. For my ideas. And … my glasses … and some headphones from my son. He's sixteen years old.
TW: Do you have a photo? A photo of your son?
J: No, I don't. My family photos are in the living room. What else is on my desk? A plant, and … a cup of coffee. An apple …
TW: So what's different about your desk?
J: Well, I have two notebooks. A big notebook and a small notebook. Different notebooks for different things.
TW: OK, thank you Joe. And next is …

Audio 3.04
1 I have a computer and a keyboard.
2 I have a cup of coffee.
3 I don't have any pencils on my desk.
4 Joe, do you have a job?
5 Yes, I do.
6 Do you have a photo of your son?
7 No, I don't.
8 I have two notebooks.

Audio 3.05
1 Toni: Do you have a job?
  Joe: Yes, I do.
2 Toni: Do you have a photo of your son?
  Joe: No, I don't.

Audio 3.06
B = Becca I = Ian M = Man R = Ryan
N = Nia
Conversation 1
B: Hey Ian, look at this jacket.
I: Nice! Brown's a good colour for you. How much is it?
B: I don't know. Excuse me?
M: Can I help you?
B: Yes, how much is this jacket?
M: It's thirty pounds.
B: Can I try it on?
M: Yes, of course.
B: Thanks. It's … big. Do you have a small?
M: No, I don't.
I: It's great, Becca. It's good on you. Really.
B: OK. How about twenty-five pounds?
M: No, it's thirty.
B: OK, thirty pounds.

Conversation 2
R: Are you online?
N: Yeah, I'm on sportsclub101.com.
R: Do they have jumpers?
N: No, it's all sports clothes. Oh wait, yes, they have jumpers.
R: Great.
N: Um, yeah. What size are you? Medium?
R: No, large.

N: Large, OK. What colour? They have green, blue and black.
R: Blue … Is it dark blue?
N: Yes, it is.
R: Then blue. How much is it?
N: Forty-nine pounds.
R: OK. Fine.
N: Anything else? I have your jumper and a top for me.
R: That's fine.
N: OK. Where's your credit card?
R: My credit card?
N: Yeah. My credit card is in the bedroom.
R: Oh, OK. My credit card is on the table.
N: Got it, thanks.

Audio 3.07
I = Ian B = Becca M = Man
R = Ryan N = Nia
1 I: How much is it?
  B: I don't know. Excuse me?
  M: Can I help you?
  B: Yes, how much is this jacket? … Can I try it on?
  M: Yes, of course.
2 N: What size are you? Medium?
  R: No, large. …
     Is it dark blue?
  N: Yes, it is.
  R: Then blue. How much is it?

Audio 3.08
1a Excuse me.
1b Excuse me.
2a How much is this jacket?
2b How much is this jacket?
3a Can I try it on?
3b Can I try it on?

UNIT 3 VOCABULARY BANK

Audio VB3.01
A red
B yellow
C blue
D green
E white
F black
G brown
H orange
I purple
J pink

Audio VB3.02
1 It's a dark blue bus.
2 It's a light blue bus.
3 They're light brown.
4 It's dark red.

Audio VB3.03
A top
B trousers
C skirt
D suit
E shoes
F jacket
G coat
H T-shirt
I jumper
J dress
K shirt
L jeans

Audio VB3.04
A shoe shop
B bookshop
C sports shop
D clothes shop
E supermarket
F baker's
G butcher's
H pet shop
I video game shop
J computer shop

UNIT 3 REVIEW

Audio R3.01
I have a travel blog and every weekend I go to a new city. It's important for me to travel with a very small bag! I have extra clothes – two shirts, a jumper for cold evenings and a jacket for rain. I don't have my laptop – I love it, but it's really big, so I have a notebook and a pen. It's my favourite pen – a present from my parents. And I have sticky notes in different colours – yellow for information about food, blue for hotels and green for transport. And I have a phone with a great camera. That's it!

UNIT 3 SOUNDS AND SPELLING

Audio S3.01
/p/ pen, people, happy, cup, shop
/b/ bank, bed, baby, website, job
/k/ camera, coffee, jacket, black, think
/g/ girl, goodbye, guitar, big, bag
/t/ T-shirt, waiter, letter, suit, what
/d/ doctor, dark, address, red, bad

Audio S3.02
1 It's a pea.
2 It's a bee.
3 It's a bee.
4 It's a pea.
5 It's a bee.
6 It's a pea.
7 It's cold.
8 It's gold.
9 It's cold.
10 It's cold.
11 It's gold.
12 It's gold.
13 town
14 down
15 town
16 down
17 down
18 town

Audio S3.03
1 cup, cup of, a cup of coffee
2 job, job in, a job in town
3 think, think it's, I think it's great.
4 bag, bag of, a bag of bananas
5 what, what are, What are your names?
6 good, good answer, a good answer
7 love, love it, I love it.
8 like, like it, I don't like it.

165

AUDIOSCRIPTS

UNIT 4

Audio 4.01
1. egg, fish, rice, steak
2. apple, chicken, mushroom, pasta, sandwich
3. banana, tomato

Audio 4.02
I = Isabel   M = Miki   A = Aiden

I: My husband is Italian. In Italy, we usually have lunch together in our apartment: my two children, my husband and my husband's mother. We eat together. We always have pasta for lunch. Pasta and tomatoes or pasta and mushrooms and cheese. After the pasta we have meat or fish. Fish is our favourite. Then we often eat fruit, an apple or a banana. We drink water with lunch and after lunch, we drink coffee. I love coffee.

M: For lunch I have a 'bento' box, or Japanese lunch box. I make different food every day. I usually have rice, fish or chicken and vegetables. What do I have in my box today? My box has rice, an egg, tomatoes and other vegetables. After lunch I always drink tea, green tea, every day.

A: Lunch? Well, I don't often eat a big lunch. In the morning I make a sandwich. I really like cheese sandwiches or egg sandwiches. I sometimes eat my sandwich at my desk or I sometimes go to the park. Then I have an apple. I love apples. After lunch I drink a cup of tea. Always tea. I never drink coffee. I hate it.

Audio 4.03
1. makes
2. gets up
3. writes
4. leaves
5. goes
6. listens
7. finishes
8. watches

Audio 4.04
W = waiter   C = customer

Conversation 1
W: Can I help you?
C: Yes. Can I have a coffee, please?
W: With milk and sugar?
C: Just milk, thank you.
W: OK, a coffee with milk. Here you go.
C: How much is that?
W: That's three pounds.
C: Thanks.

Conversation 2
C: Hi.
W: Hi.
C: Can I have a tea and a pastry, please?
W: Yes, just a moment. Here you are.
C: Thank you. Oh, can I have a fork, please?
W: It's on the table.
C: Oh yes. Thank you.
W: Anything else?
C: No, thank you. How much is that?
W: Erm, that's four pounds eighty.
C: Four pounds eighty.
W: Thank you.

Conversation 3
C: Excuse me. What's the breakfast special today?
W: The breakfast specials are here, on the menu.
C: OK … So a sandwich and a coffee is five pounds fifty?
W: Yes, a sandwich and a coffee … or a tea.
C: Great. Can I have the sandwich breakfast special, please?
W: Coffee or tea?
C: Coffee, please.
W: Coffee. Anything else?
C: Oh, can I have a mineral water, please?
W: Still or sparkling?
C: Oh, sparkling, please. How much is that?
W: Just a moment. Let me check. One sandwich breakfast special with a coffee, and a sparkling mineral water.
C: Yes.
W: That's … seven pounds fifty.

Audio 4.05
W = waiter   C = customer
W: Can I help you?
C: Yes. Can I have a coffee, please?
W: OK, a coffee with milk. Here you go.
C: How much is that?
W: That's three pounds.
C: Can I have a tea and a pastry, please?
W: Yes, just a moment. Here you are.
W: Anything else?
C: No, thank you.
W: Coffee or tea?
C: Coffee, please.
W: Still or sparkling?
C: Oh, sparkling, please. How much is that?
W: Just a moment. Let me check.

Audio 4.06
Coffee or tea?

Audio 4.07
A: OK, ask me questions.
B: Let me see. OK, is it a man or a woman?
A: A woman. And now it's easy for you.
B: Not so easy. Does she work in a hospital?
A: No, she doesn't.
B: Does she work outdoors?
A: Yes, sometimes.
B: Does she drive in her job?
A: Yes, she does.
B: OK, she doesn't work in a hospital, so she isn't a nurse. She sometimes works outdoors and she drives in her job.
A: So, who is it?
B: Hmm. The bus driver in the photo is a man, so I think she's the police officer.
A: You're right. Now it's my turn.

UNIT 4 VOCABULARY BANK

Audio VB4.01
Fruit: apple, banana, orange
Vegetables: carrot, mushroom, potato, tomato
Meat: steak, beef, chicken
Drinks: milk, fruit juice
Other: pasta, fish, bread, cereal, rice, cheese, egg, sandwich

Audio VB4.02
A ten o'clock
B quarter past ten
C half past ten
D quarter to eleven
E eleven o'clock

Audio VB4.03
A cup
B glass
C fork
D plate
E knife
F spoon
G bowl
H chopsticks
I napkin
J sugar
K salt
L pepper

UNIT 4 REVIEW

Audio R4.01
What do you eat?
I eat five times every day, not really five meals, sometimes it's just a snack. In the morning at six, I have a banana and some chocolate and then I have training. For breakfast I always have five eggs and some fruit. At half past ten, I have breakfast number two, but nothing big, for example a bowl of cereal with milk. I sometimes have a sandwich for lunch, or I have pasta. Dinner is usually at quarter to seven. I often have a steak with rice, cheese and two or three vegetables, maybe a potato, some carrots and some tomatoes. I love ice cream, but I never eat it – not before a race!

UNIT 4 SOUNDS AND SPELLING

Audio S4.01
/e/ egg, pepper, get, never, twelve
/æ/ apple, carrot, napkin, hat, Africa
/ʌ/ mushroom, lunch, sometimes, love, mother

Audio S4.02
1. cap, cup
2. hat, hut
3. man, men

Audio S4.03
cap, cup, hat, cap, cup, men, man, cap, men, hat, man, men, hat, hut, hut, hat

Audio S4.04
1. breakfast, We have breakfast at seven.
2. young, Nate is very young, only two years old.
3. headphones, Where are my headphones?
4. friend, That's my friend Amy.
5. one, It's one o'clock.
6. any, Do you have any eggs?
7. again, Can you say it again, please?
8. country, In my country we speak Spanish.

Audio S4.05
A: Does your classroom have a computer?
B: Yes, it does.
A: Does it have a blackboard?
B: No, it doesn't. It has a whiteboard.

VIDEOSCRIPTS

UNIT 1

Opener: BBC Vlogs
1 Hi, I'm Beatriz and I'm from Portugal.
2 Hello, my name is Mo. I come from China.
3 Hi, my name's Anna. I'm from Queensland, Australia.
4 Hi. My name's Brian. I'm from the United States.
5 My name's Kayo. I'm from Japan.
6 Hi, I'm Phil. I'm from England.
7 Hi, I'm Holly and I'm from Nottingham in England.
8 Hi. My name is Daniel. I'm from Poland.
9 Hello. My name is Sonia and I'm from Serbia.
10 My name's Lucia. I'm from Spain.

1D: BBC Street Interviews
Exs 2A and 2B

William: My name is William and it's spelt W-I-L-L-I-A-M.
Rachael: My name is Rachael. R-A-C-H-A-E-L.
Chris: My name is Chris. C-H-R-I-S.
Sharron: Sharron. And that's S-H-A, double-R, O-N.
Ian: My name's Ian. That is spelt I-A-N.
Simnit: Simnit, and it's spelt S-I-M-N-I-T.
Biba: My first name is Biba, and I spell it B-I-B-A.
Layan: So it's Layan, and it's L-A-Y-A-N.
Tom: My name is Tom. That's T-O-M.

Exs 3A and 3C

William: I have a sandwich in my bag.
Rachael: I have a bottle of water. I have my purse, my keys.
Chris: I have a laptop and a notebook.
Sharron: I have a bottle of water, a notebook and a banana.
Ian: I have a laptop and a mobile.
Simnit: I have an umbrella, my mobile phone and my purse.
Biba: In my bag I have my phone and my wallet.
Layan: So I have my wallet and some make-up.
Tom: I have my laptop and two books.

UNIT 2

Opener: BBC Vlogs
1 Hello. My name is Jorge. I'm from Colombia. Today, I am in Bogotá.
2 Hi, I'm Sherri. I'm from California. Now, I'm in New York.
3 Hi, I'm Alison. I'm from Scotland, but now I'm in Italy.
4 Hello. My name is Anastasia. I'm American and Russian. Today I'm in London.
5 Hello. My name's Iullia and I'm from Russia. I live in Italy, in Rome.
6 Hello. I'm Rory. I'm from England. I'm now in Ireland.
7 Hello. My name is Hanan Ali. I'm from Mombasa, Kenya, and I'm currently in Columbus, Ohio.
8 Hi. I'm Jennifer. I'm from Australia, but now I'm in Florence in Italy.
9 Hi. I'm Fotis. I'm from Greece. I'm now in Madrid, Spain.

2D: BBC Food
Exs 2B, 2C and 2D

N = Narrator   Cl = Claudia   R = Robin   E = Elisabetta
Ch = Chris   M = Mary   A = Angela

N: Ten home cooks. Eight weeks. Twenty-four tasks. Three judges. This is *Best Home Cook*. It's Week four. The home cooks arrive.
Cl: Hi. Hello.
R: Hi, Claudia.
E: Good morning.
N: Our presenter is Claudia Winkleman.
Cl: How are we all?
All: Good, good.
N: Next, the judges arrive.
Cl: Judges!
J: Morning!
All: Morning.
N: It's time for today's task.
Cl: You have three hours to make the ultimate birthday cake. Let's go.
N: The task is a children's birthday cake. Robin is 63. He's a manager from Bristol in the UK. He has a wife and a daughter. Suzie is 36. She has two children and she's from Northern Ireland. Georgia is 24 years old and she's from London. She's a model. Oli is a manager in a restaurant. He's 34 and he's married. He and his wife have one daughter. Katie's 33. She's married and she works in a supermarket. Elisabetta is 52. She's from Italy, but now her home is in London. Sarah's 42 and has a son. They're from Manchester.
Cl: Fifteen minutes! One minute, cooks. And that's it, time's up.
N: Finally, the cakes are finished. But are they good? So, who are the three winners?
Ch: And that is… Suzie's.
M: The one that stood out for me… It was Robin's.
A: Katie, well done.
N: And now it's time to rest before next week.

UNIT 3

Opener: BBC Vlogs
1 My favourite thing is my garden. In the summer, it's beautiful.
2 My dog. His name is Jasper. He is a labradoodle.
3 My favourite thing is my bike. It's new. I love it because it's green and yellow and it's really fast.
4 My favourite thing is my teddy bear. His name is Fred.
5 My favourite thing is this painting of Venice in Italy.
6 My favourite thing is my camera. This is a Canon digital camera.
7 My favourite thing is my bicycle.
8 My new red car. It's great!

3D: BBC Street Interviews
Exs 2A and 2C

Rachael: I buy food online and I buy make-up and clothes in shops.
Elijah: I buy things for the house online.
Gloria: I buy clothes online and I buy food in shops.
Joe: Online I buy video games and in shops I buy food.
Josh: Online I buy clothes and in shops I also buy food.
Holly: I buy make-up online and I buy food in shops.
Nic: I buy cat food online. I buy clothes in shops.
Kirsty: I buy books online and I buy shoes in the shop.
Vincent: I buy trainers online.

Exs 3A and 3B

Rachael: I love clothes shops, I hate butchers and I love cafés.
Elijah: I like restaurants, I like cafés, and I like supermarkets.
Gloria: I love clothes shops, and I hate sports shops.
Joe: I like sports shops, and I dislike clothes shops.
Josh: I like food shops, because I like food, and I don't like pet shops.
Holly: I like clothes shops. I don't like bookshops.
Nic: I like food shops. I do not like clothes shops.
Kirsty: I like clothes shops and shoe shops, and I dislike computer shops.
Vincent: I like video game shops.

UNIT 4

Opener: BBC Vlogs
1 My favourite meal is lunch. I always have tuna salad.
2 My favourite meal is dinner. I love fish.
3 Breakfast is my favourite meal. I always have coffee and fruit.
4 My favourite meal is dinner. I eat a lot of pasta with cheese.
5 My favourite meal of the day is breakfast. I have an omelette with a cup of tea.
6 My favourite meal is breakfast. I have cereal with milk, and orange juice.
7 Lunch. My favourite, er, food is pasta. I love Italian food.
8 My favourite meal is breakfast. I have breakfast at my desk. I have eggs and two cups of coffee.

VIDEOSCRIPTS

4D: BBC Documentary
Exs 2B and 2C
N = Narrator   B = Billy   E = Elvira

N: From space we can see colours and shapes … water … and land. Zoom in and we can see many different lives.

In the city of Chennai in India, thousands of parakeets eat breakfast. This is Joseph Sekar's house. He gets up at half past five every morning and makes rice for the parakeets. He puts the rice out and waits. The first parakeet comes at six o'clock in the morning. Four thousand parakeets come to his home every day. Joseph loves the parakeets. He says, 'All living things are important.'

In Colorado, in the USA, Billy Ellis gets up early.

B: I get up, have a cup of coffee and then I'm ready to go.

N: He climbs 143 steps … to his office. Forest fires are a big problem in Colorado. Billy is a fire lookout. He watches the forest for fires. It's a difficult job. Does he see many forest fires? No, not often, but when he sees a fire, it's his job to call the firefighters.

In the north of Peru, in a national park, we can see Lake El Dorado. Elvira is nine years old. She lives in a small village near Lake El Dorado. She goes to school there. Elvira loves animals. Her favourite animals … are manatees. Manatees usually live in rivers. But sometimes they need a new home. Today is a special day. Some men bring a manatee to live in the lake. Elvira sees a manatee for the first time. She's really happy. The men put the manatee into the lake. It has a new home. Elvira watches the manatee and says goodbye.

E: Chau manatee!

VERB TABLE

REGULAR VERBS

infinitive	he/she/it	past simple
answer	answers	answered
arrive	arrives	arrived
ask	asks	asked
book	books	booked
call	calls	called
change	changes	changed
check	checks	checked
clean	cleans	cleaned
close	closes	closed
dance	dances	danced
finish	finishes	finished
help	helps	helped
like	likes	liked
listen	listens	listened
live	lives	lived
look	looks	looked
love	loves	loved
match	matches	matched
meet	meets	met
open	opens	opened
plan	plans	planned
play	plays	played
relax	relaxes	relaxed
remember	remembers	remembered
say	says	said
see	sees	saw
send	sends	sent
sleep	sleeps	slept
spend	spends	spent
start	starts	started
stay	stays	stayed
take	takes	took
thank	thanks	thanked
travel	travels	travelled
try	tries	tried
use	uses	used
visit	visits	visited
walk	walks	walked
want	wants	wanted
wash	washes	washed
watch	watches	watched
work	works	worked

IRREGULAR VERBS

infinitive	he/she/it	past simple
be	is	was
buy	buys	bought
choose	chooses	chose
come	comes	came
do	does	did
feed	feeds	fed
get	gets	got
give	gives	gave
go	goes	went
have	has	had
know	knows	knew
leave	leaves	left
make	makes	made
say	says	said
send	sends	sent
understand	understands	understood
write	writes	wrote

Pearson Education Limited
KAO Two
KAO Park
Hockham Way
Harlow, Essex
CM17 9SR
England
and Associated Companies throughout the world.

pearson.com/languages

© Pearson Education Limited 2023

All rights reserved; no part of this publication may be reproduced, stored in a retrieval system, or transmitted in any form or by any means, electronic, mechanical, photocopying, recording, or otherwise without the prior written permission of the Publishers.

First published 2023

ISBN: 978-1-292-41853-7

Set in BBC Reith Sans

Printed and bound by Ashford Colour Press

Acknowledgements
Written by Frances Eales and Steve Oakes.
The publishers and authors would like to thank the following people for their feedback and comments during the development of the material:
Charlotte Buckmaster, Sally Gayford, Charlotte A. Gerard, Billie Jago, Dorota Walesiak.

Image Credits:
123RF.com: 123rfaurinko 126, 1xpert 44, afefelov68 133, agcreativelab 130, Andrei Tselichtchev 126, belchonock 135, Bogdan Ionescu 139, Dmitriy Shironosov 133, Edie Layland 132, foodandmore 6, Georgii Dolgykh 152, Jacek Chabraszewski 131, jenoche 130, jose maria hernandez 6, lightpoet 133, Milosh Kojadinovich 126, Olga Yastremska 129, otosylvie 129, Pan Xunbin 153, Petar Djordjevic 128, picsfive 129, runna 134, Ruth Black 129, serezniy 139, Sergey Dzyuba 139, Sergey Kolesnikov 153, Shao-Chun Wang 6, stockyimages 133, Wavebreak Media Ltd 125, Yongyut Khasawong 14; **Alamy Stock Photo:** H. Mark Weidman Photography 19, imageBROKER 135, Nigel Hicks 146, 149; **BBC Studios:** 7, 14, 15, 17, 24, 25, 27, 34, 35, 37, 44, 47, 54, 55, 57, 64, 67, 74, 75, 77, 84, 85, 150; **Getty Images:** 10'000 Hours/DigitalVision 32, 48, 125, A-S-L/E+ 132, AleksandarNakic/E+ 68, Alexander Spatari/Moment 42, 60, 67, 122, alvarez/E+ 12, 138, AndreyPopov/iStock 59, Andrii Lutsyk/Ascent Xmedia/Stone 57, ArtMarie/E+ 32, AzmanL/E+ 63, Basak Gurbuz Derman/Moment 137, Betsie Van Der Meer/Stone 130, bortonia/DigitalVision Vectors 151, 155, 158, BrianAJackson/iStock 48, Bulgac/E+ 28, Burak Karademir/Moment 9, Carol Yepes/Moment 105, CasarsaGuru/iStock 78, Catherine Falls Commercial/Moment 127, Christopher A. Jones/Moment Open 62, Cohen/Ostrow/Digital Vision 10, Compassionate Eye Foundation/Natasha Alipour Faridani/Digital Vision 125, Cultura RM Exclusive/Quim Roser/Publisher Mix 82, daboost/iStock 124, 126, David Maln/Stone 29, Dean Mitchell/E+ 81, Delmaine Donson/E+ 147, digitalskillet/iStock 140, 143, dowel/Moment China 52, drbimages/iStock 137, dub303 102, eclipse_images/E+ 68, EdwardShtern/iStock 129, Edwin Tan/E+ 46, Emma Innocenti/DigitalVision 21, energyy/iStock 137, Ernesto r. Ageitos/Moment 124, Eugenio Marongiu/Image Source 7, Eva-Katalin/E+ 124, Explora_2005/iStock 130, Ezra Bailey/The Image Bank 37, ferrantraite/E+ 79, FG Trade/iStock 140, 143, FilippoBacci 140, fotografixx/E+ 60, franckreporter/iStock 13, Gary John Norman/The Image Bank 139, Gary Yeowell/Stone 112, GCShutter/ E+ 133, George Mdivanian/EyeEm 137, Glowimages 139, Graham Montanari/iStock 137, Halfpoint/iStock 30, Henrik Sorensen/DigitalVision 26, Hill Street Studios/DigitalVision 119, Hinterhaus Productions/DigitalVision 6, 125, ideeone/E+ 66, Indeed 32, Ismail Kaya/EyeEm 104, itsskin/E+ 60, izusek/E+ 52, 52, J Shepherd/Photographers Choice RF 110, Jacobs Stock Photography Ltd/DigitalVision 76, JakeOlimb/ DigitalVision Vectors 153, Jakkapan Jabjainai/EyeEm 28, Jens Benscheidt/EyeEm 140, 143, Joe Daniel Price/Moment 78, 83, Johannes Mann/The Image Bank 92, John Giustina/The Image Bank 135, John Keeble/Moment 134, JohnFScott/E+ 18, Jon Feingersh Photography Inc/DigitalVision 116, Jose Luis Pelaez Inc/Digital Vision 136, Juan Mabromata/AFP 71, Julien McRoberts 107, Justin Ford/Getty Images Sport 146, 149, K505/iStock 28, kali9/E+ 8, Kentaroo Tryman/Maskot 124, Kontrec/E+ 72, Leadinglights iStock 135, Letizia Le Fur/ONOKY 138, LightFieldStudios/iStock 125, Luis Alvarez/DigitalVision 94, making_ultimate/Moment 139, manbophoto/iStock 84-85, mapodile/E+ 82, Marco Bottigelli/Moment 17, martin-dm/E+ 114, Maskot 23, 38, 127, 143, Matej Kastelic/EyeEm 50, Matteo Colombo/Moment 10, Meiko Arquillos/UpperCut Images 30, Meinzahn/iStock 136, mevans/E+ 136, Michael H/Stone 136, Michael Roberts/Moment 19, Mint Images 124, 134, mladn61/iStock 128, monkeybusinessimages/iStock 125, Monty Rakusen/Image Source 47, monzenmachi/E+ 21, 88, Morsa Images/DigitalVision 125, Morsa Images/Stone 154, Nikada/E+ 22, Norbert Kamil Kowaczek/EyeEm 38, Oliver Rossi/DigitalVision 127, Oliver Rossi/Stone 20, Pattarisara Suvichanarakul/EyeEm 137, Paul Burns/DigitalVision 135, PeopleImages/iStock 73, 106, 111, 137, 144, pixelfit/E+ 140, 143, pjohnson1/iStock 132, Portra /E+ 154, Renate Frost/EyeEm 131, Rizauddin Ibrahim/EyeEm 68, Robbie Jack 70, Robert Daly/ OJO Images 136, Roberto Machado Noa/Moment 13, runna10/iStock 78, Sakchai Vongsasiripat/Moment 130, Santiago Urquijo/E+ 82, SDI Productions/E+ 52, Sellwell/Moment 98, SementsovaLesia/iStock 36, SeventyFour/iStock 58, skynesher/E+ 125, SolStock/E+ 60, 78, SrdjanPav/iStock 29, Stephen Hathaway/EyeEm 139, Stígur Már Karlsson/Heimsmyndir/E+ 138, Stockbyte 29, Supoj Buranaprapapong/Moment 68, TheCrimsonMonkey/E+ 126, Thomas Barwick/DigitalVision 138, 138, 138, Tom Werner/DigitalVision 88, torwai/iStock 136, TravelCouples/Moment 124, Trevor Williams/DigitalVision 138, undefined undefined/iStock 137, UpperCut Images 20, Virojt Changyencham 42, vm/E+ 138, Vostok/Moment 135, webphotographeer/E+ 130, Westend61 20, 23, 28, 28, 77, 130, xavierarnau/E+ 82, 140, Yevhenii Podshyvalov/iStock 134, yongyuan/E+ 130, ziggy_mars/iStock 133; **Pearson Education Ltd:** Gareth Boden 135; **Shutterstock:** 125, 06photo 124, 132, 1000 Words 135, 166657 130, Adisa 14, Africa Studio 14, 135, Akifyeva S 153, Alberto Zamorano 135, Alex Staroseltsev 131, Angel_Vasilev77 136, anmbph 65, Anton-Burakov 126, aquatic creature 126, Asia Images Group 127, AtlasStudio 38, B Calkins 131, Belinda Pretorius 137, Billion Photos 124, blvdone 127, 127, Bokeh Blur Background Subject 153, Bondar Illia 127, Bozena Fulawka 131, BrAt82 27, Catarina Belova 65, chinahbzyg 137, 152, Coprid 154, Dani Vincek 131, Danny Smythe 132, Denis Kuvaev 127, Dionisvera 131, Dmitriy Krasko 131, Dragon Images 124, elenovsky 129, Elnur 33, 129, Faber14 88, FabrikaSimf 136, fad82 14, Ferenc Szelepcsenyi 135, foodonwhite 131, g215 14, GaudiLab 40, 41, George Rudy 130, gresei 131, Gunnar Pippel 129, homydesign 154, Hryshchyshen Serhii 10, Iasha 129, IM_photo 139, Ivanko80 80, JeniFoto 64-65, jocic 131, Juanan Barros Moreno 139, Kamil Macniak 11, Karkas 129, Kiev.Victor 65, 65, Larich 124, Leonid Ikan 153, Leyasw 20-21, Liudmyla Chuhunova 30, loskutnikov 65, LUMIKK555 68, Magdanatka 38, MaraZe 131, Masami.K 19, mavo 125, Media Union 154, Melica 29, Mohamed Rageh 136, Moving Moment 131, mukura 137, Mustafa Ertugral 152, Nataliia K 126, Nataliya Nazarova 140, 143, Nattakorn_Maneerat 8, NDanko 30, Nick Starichenko 135, notYourBusiness 128, NYS 33, Odua Images 154, Ollyy 137, oneinchpunch 143, Orlando_Stocker 14, Pavel L Photo and Video 135, Pavel1964 75, Potapov Alexander 126, ppa 134, praphab louilarpprasert 6, Rido 140, 143, Rob Wilson 128, Roman Voloshyn 10, S-F. 139, sagir 129, saiko3p 153, Samokhin 131, schankz 137, sevenke 6, Siyapath 14, SOMMAI 131, spaxiax 131, tarzhanova 129, 129, Tatiana Popova 126, 126, 131, Tatjana Romanova 137, TerraceStudio 126, Tim UR 131, Timmary 126, Tyler Olson 136, Valentin Ivantsov 129, Vereshchagin Dmitry 135, Walter Bilotta 131, WAYHOME studio 133, William Barton 61, Wong Yu Liang 137, xpixel 152, xshot 133, Zurbagan 131

Cover Images: *Front:* Alamy Stock Photo: Indiapicture; Getty Images: Brothers91, Luis Alvarez, MoMo Productions

Illustrated by: Stephen Collins (Central Illustration Agency) 24, 72, 87, 99, 103, 109, 116, 118, 119, 123; Ben Hasler (NB Illustration) 26, 51, 53, 58, 62, 80, 86, 113, 114r, 124, 136, 144b, 147b, 157, 159; Matt Hollins (Illustration X) 42; Clementine Hope (NB Illustration) 38, 43, 56, 145b; Sam Kalda (Folio) 66, 95, 100, 115, 144t, 147t; Liz Kay (NB Illustration) 63, 65; 101, 112; Andrew Pagram (Beehive Illustration) 141, 142; Szilvia Szaskill (Beehive Illustration) 9, 40, 97, 114l, 127, 145t, 148; Mark Willey (Designers Educational) 14, 59, 128, 132, 133.

Notes

Notes

Notes

Notes

Notes

Notes

Notes

Notes

Notes

Notes

Notes

Notes